2022 LONGHORN FOOTBALL PROSPECTUS

THINKING TEXAS FOOTBALL

PAUL WADLINGTON

Contents

Greetings!

Welcome to the 10th annual 2022 Longhorn Football Prospectus: Thinking Texas Football. This book is a Texas football preview, a Big 12 season companion and reference guide, and a resource for the entire 2022 football season.

Thinking Texas Football, in deference to its name, is written for an intelligent football layperson. It won't insult you by writing down to the lowest common denominator nor will it try to overawe you with technical babble. The book's best ambition is to provide you with different tools – while plainly communicating an awareness of its own biases and blind spots – so that we can engage in a conversation that mutually enriches our shared passion.

If you want to see this preview continue to be published, please write a 5 star review and share it with your tribe on social media. Sharing it and recommending it to others will guarantee future editions. This book can't continue without your support!

Hook 'em!

The Brave New World Of College Football

Strauss-Howe generational theory, whether one finds it kooky or clarifying, posits that there are decades in human history that feel like weeks and that there are weeks that feel like decades. College football just went through a few weeks with more fundamental structural change than the four decades prior. The structure of the game, the fan experience, the nature of amateurism, an individual's right to own one's own name, image, and likeness, and the very connection that universities, their alumni, and their sports teams share have been called into question, utterly transforming the landscape, even the conception of college athletics.

Will a culture that already too often celebrates me over we be improved by paying 18 year olds large amounts of money and easing their transfer to the next opportunity the moment they hit a smidgen of adversity? How can a program alchemize the athlete's desire "to build out their brand" into wins on Saturday? Now more than ever, a program must stress common goals built less on feel-good school loyalty and more on shared mutual interest. An early caution to the reader: feelings about these changes are likely as useful as one's feelings about the law of gravity. You are welcome to them, but gravity doesn't need anyone's approval. Just understand that stairs are a better conveyance than a window. Or don't. Use the window, flap your arms, believe really hard, and see how it works out. This article deals with how things are and will be, not wishcasting.

The explosion of NIL money means a brave new world for college football and its athletes. An evolution that will only highlight the imperative of building, enforcing, reshaping, and inculcating culture while navigating a lucrative landscape of incentives. Developing a realistic, clear-eyed, flexible and durable culture is the only lid on the Pandora's Box of NIL. Outside of the locker room, the de facto professionalization of amateur sports will also have massive impacts on fan and media perception and behaviors with accompanying exigent pressures. Right now, being a scholarship offensive linemen at the University of Texas is worth upwards of 150K per year. That number will grow. How will that fact influence fan tolerance for a bad game from the right tackle? Similarly, the sponsored professionalization of amateur sports means that treating 19 and 20 year olds as "kids" isn't going to fly anymore. Leeway for emotional and expectational allowances once granted generously and automatically are now contingent on performance. College athletes have always been criticized, but there was always a degree of measured restraint. These were "our kids." But how about when the kids can publicly shop for wealthier parents and transfer to a new family living in a better house that does not enforce a curfew? Still your kids? When athletes are paid like employees, they will be expected to perform like one. Even if the athlete's emotional infrastructure isn't ready for it.

The taboos against booing college football players or lauding under-talented Timmy for trying his best in a failing effort will fade. With greater reward will come greater scrutiny and an accompanying fan and media sense that college players should be treated the same as the professionals. Not everyone will become quite as obnoxious as Philadelphia Eagles fans, but the exchanges between college fan and athlete will be much more transactional, conditional, and less sentimental. The days of hiding behind the skirt of "student-athlete" are numbered. In late June of this year, new Florida head coach Billy Napier called four Gator football players into his office and unceremoniously cut them. Florida had four scholarships over the 85 limit and needed to trim up by August. The coaches cut the fat. Traditionalists were aghast and retired to their fainting couches. Just two years earlier, Napier might have handled that differently, counseling those athletes to transfer after a frank assessment of their position on the depth chart, perhaps offering a face-saving medical scholarship to remove them from the roster but allow them to keep school paid for, or simply telling them that the staff did not see them in their future plans and let the athletes figure it out. But NIL has changed the landscape so quickly that coaches no longer need a pretext. Hey fellas, you're fired. Pack up your stuff. Here is a Greyhound bus ticket and a ham sandwich. The quaint folkways of a time past are dead and buried. And by a time past, we mean the ancient days of 2019.

A scholarship is no longer just free housing and food, a free education, endless resources, and top notch facilities. It is all of that plus a potential six figure salary. For some, millions. We will see players routinely transfer three or more times in one collegiate career seeking the maximization of their brand. And we will see college coaches call players into their office and tell them they are no longer needed in Gainesville, Norman, Columbus or Austin. The opportunity cost of a misallocated scholarship is now greater for a school that can compete for (and buy) the best talent through recruiting and portal alike. In fact, the fluidity of the portal now means that it's simply an extension of the high school recruiting process. Any team that does not have a dedicated internal scouting arm devoted to other college programs – separate from high schools, JUCO, or opponent scouting – is foolish. The most immediate fix to a problem on your defense is not playing high school ball. The most immediate fix is the underpaid Conference USA defensive player of the year, whose NIL consists of a local porta potty broker and a sod wholesaler. While minor programs will be mercilessly robbed of their stars, smarter FCS and lower tier FBS programs will allow elite programs to feed them interesting prospects that they like but do not have room for with the understanding that they will circle back and take them if that player turns into a superstar. Whether he does or does not, at minimum, the lesser program has a very talented rental it otherwise would not have had for two or three years.

Fans and coaches will have less patience in how to get better performance out of Player X. Instead of asking – how can we break through to that player? – they will now ask: who might we have instead? Why learn to play your cards optimally when you can draw new ones? Roster tampering happens now, but it is about to find a bull market. In a college environment with no salary cap and roster limits that can be manipulated through NIL dollars to walk-ons, the potential for mischief is extraordinary. Schools that are not building out a strong scouting and back channel recruiting apparatus for other team's rosters will be left behind.

So what does that mean for "non-performing" scholarship players?

It used to be that a marginal performer with program buy-in who took care of business off of the field and with no desire to transfer out for playing time was generally kept on scholarship. It was an unwritten cultural rule, an underpinning of team chemistry and loyalty. Some unsentimental SEC powers (cough, Alabama, cough) mastered the convenient medical scholarship and a soft trapdoor so those players could save face ("We're pretty sure your mildly sprained shoulder prevents you from ever playing again, but by all means stick around and get your degree"), but plenty of schools carried their program guys through to the end. What about now? Will that athlete be treated the same? He's "wasting" a spot. A scholarship with much greater implied value since there are now more options to fill it. Getting rid of a marginal performer who has no buy-in has always been easy. But what about the good citizens who give all for the king and country that can be ruthlessly upgraded? Expect an increasingly unsentimental vitality curve to be enforced.

College football players currently struggle to focus without receiving cash for being on the team. Well, legal cash. A generation that derives much of their validation and emotional health from strangers on social media now must honor that social media as a brand-building tool that puts dollars in their pockets. How is a teen's focus going to be affected by six figure income, almost no expenses, dubious maturity, and meager financial literacy? Now add intense adulation, worship, hatred, venom, useless hangers ons and parasites – all of the digital impostors guised as triumph and disaster. Not to mention the increased potential for dealing with friends and family who will reveal their true colors as exploiters and opportunists at a formative age. Though now, interestingly, the college player being paid directly once he enrolls may actually disempower some of the blatant auctions and middlemen. The smart players will shut down the street agents who take their 80% and then trickle the rest to the athlete. NIL has financially disempowered the uncle, personal trainer, or head coach middleman. Right now, there are college recruiters creating pitch decks like an advertising executive about to have a client pitch with Budweiser.

Fans aren't typically paragons of patience. What about booster patience paying directly into a non-performing product? It is one thing to hope for results because of time and emotional investment, donations, and season tickets. It is quite another when one is cutting checks directly to players and the product remains unacceptable. The wealthier the program, the more the potentially corrupting influence, so the greater the need for clear-eyed coaches to build out a viable program culture durable enough to weather the increasingly mercenary reality of NIL. The coaches who build a viable locker room will look more to the NFL than college for their model. However, they will be without the NFL tools of legally enforced contracts with fines for non-compliance or a salary cap. A lot of folks in the SEC, including one Saint Nicholas Saban, wished that Texas A&M had a salary cap for their 2022 recruiting class. However, as the Billy Napier roster cut story illustrates, the professional mentality, even without all of the tools, is coming to college sports. The mental evaluation of players – already paramount – is now everything.

This brings to head the NCAA and the journalistic initiative to govern and limit NIL free agency, tampering, and open bidding wars for college talent.

The NCAA used to be in charge. Well, sort of. Any government rules by the consent of the governed. Whether manufactured through consensus and an appeal to common interests, honest power exchange, or manipulation and coercion. But no governance can continue if the governed simply say enough. The NCAA long ruled universities by virtue of a common consensus amongst the governed institutions. Outlaw behavior was generally understood and defined and the vast majority of universities – those inconvenient academic institutions attached to football teams – fretted and worried about being branded renegades. That was the NCAA's power: isolation, shame, reprobation. Fully derived from the consent of those it governed. The NCAA, in its institutional bureaucratic arrogance, came to believe that its power was derived from its simple existence. Such is the nature of all bureaucracy.

We have entered a new era. Universities and their athletic programs have become increasingly unmoored. College football no longer has to honor most of its pretenses. The NCAA was made irrelevant as those it purports to lead created alternative practices and adopted a different outlook. Forced by legal rulings, Have/Have Not sorting, and de facto athletic free agency. Censure loses its power when shame is removed from the game. The question then, is not one of NCAA authority. It is whether the institutions themselves wish to curb NIL, portal hopping, and tampering excesses to save the core elements of the sport. The NCAA will be used as the convenient tool to enforce this consensus, but they are not in charge. The real power dynamic is between the major conferences fueled by live television rights in an uneasy tension with those it purports to govern: the athletes.

There is already ample "wet streets cause rain" journalism suggesting that the NCAA is driving change. They are not in charge. They are a vehicle. The NCAA is now an intermediating body to enforce conference and key team desires underwritten by television money to create distance and deniability in the real struggle between capital and labor. In the Smithian rather than Marxist sense. The athletes should be paid and should be able to realize their value. However, if they do not understand that it is the distinctive insignia on their helmets and the corresponding sense of loyalty and connection from the alums, and a larger popular identification with them as representatives of the university, regional or state brand, as central to their personal brand, then they will murder the golden goose of NIL. The hard truth is that these amazing young athletes, absent a well developed professional minor league structure that the NFL has zero interest in building, will be worth very little without the interest of college football fans. Turn the fans off enough and the NIL spigot is turned off. Name, Image, Likeness will only be relevant to an Employee of the Month sign at Home Depot. If they turn college football fans off with too much portal hopping, self promotion, and naked excess, they will find themselves playing on a semi-pro field rented from a local junior high in front of 800 instead of 80,000, sponsorship money flowing not from NIL foundations and major brands, but Chico's Bail Bonds. The athletes must have the foresight to modestly regulate themselves. Not out of kindness, but out of their own self-interest in preserving the college lie.

The coaches are getting into the action as well. They already enjoyed de facto free agency and marketing opportunities, but that is now hyper realized. Before the 2021 college football season had even reached its conclusion, five of the ten best football jobs in the country were thrown open. That's never happened before, but in this brave new world of college football free agency, one should hesitate before declaring that it will never happen again. Consider the depths and unpredictable tides of these uncharted waters. It's time to start coloring in the new maps.

The takeaway of 2021 to college administrators and coaches is a sense of urgency today or a guarantee of regret tomorrow. Never have so many significant college programs parted ways so quickly with a failing coach, or done so during the season. This preview is a proponent of always doing immediately what you'll have to do eventually and it seems that college football's power brokers, once fearful, cautious, chummy, backward-looking, have largely resigned to the same perspective. Fans are squaring themselves to that new reality as well. Coaches have now fully embraced their mercenary status, that shift reaching its ultimate realization when Urban Meyer turned it into a narcissistic art form. Messy divorces that would have dragged on for years are now being severed with Henry VIII's executional efficiency. Sentimentality shrugged off like a head on a guillotine. Athletic directors and power brokers are making sober assessments about where the head coach is today, not what he did two years prior. In turn, head coaches are learning to time their moves ahead of the posse.

LSU fired Ed Orgeron ("they reached a mutual agreement") on October 17, 2021. Just nineteen months prior, Orgeron coached the Tigers to the national title, leading a historically great team. He stumbled in 2020, doubled down on failure in 2021, and evidenced rather quickly that he could not handle success; he was a figurehead bolstered by two outstanding coordinators and an epic confluence of talent. Coach O couldn't coach or hire his way out of his predicament. Ed Orgeron sure as hell can't talk his way out of failure either. The man needs closed captioning to be understood. LSU let Orgeron finish out the season – a means of avoiding the interim head coach poison – which bought time and space to make their hire. They landed Brian Kelly, a proven veteran coach with a 113-40 record at Notre Dame. Just a decade ago, LSU could not have made a move on Orgeron until 2024. It just wasn't done. It is now.

Florida fired Dan Mullen despite season ending poll rankings of 6th, 7th, and 12th in his first three years in Gainesville. However, in late 2020, Florida's locker room fell apart, Mullen began to actively explore other options while demanding a contract extension, and the decline carried over into 2021 with a 5-6 record and a 2-6 performance in the SEC East. Florida didn't dither and pray that Mullen would regain his mojo or discover a more pleasant or loyal personality. They cut bait and their brand was damaged far less than Mullen's. In fact, their brand was damaged and Mullen came off as a disloyal narcissist. Billy Napier (32-5 over his last three seasons at Louisiana) is their relatively unproven, but enticing new way forward. Napier was well rewarded for his own impeccable timing exiting his program in Lafayette. Most thought he should have exited after 2020 to a middle tier FBS gig. Napier held on masterfully and secured a Top 10 program job. He and his agent deserve a steady golf clap for their patience in ignoring a middling climb up the ladder for a ride in a penthouse elevator.

USC fired head coach Clay Helton in September after a 42-28 loss to a poor Stanford team. Helton started encouragingly in Troy (he went 21-6 in 2016/2017) but his actual ability level caught up to his on field record. Trojan faithful wanted Helton gone last year and he was a Dead Man Coaching in 2021. Mike Bohn made his move, appointed a true interim (making it clear that the interim couldn't earn the job – the new breed of athletic director is finally learning) and bought the time and space to assess the landscape and land his guy. USC was too late in making their change, but Bohn used that time effectively to marshal the money needed to land a whale. That he did. Los Angeles, not Illinois, is now the Land of Lincoln. Why would Lincoln Riley flee Norman for Los Angeles? Perhaps he had insights about his own roster and culture that he did not like. Perhaps he understood that he would never have more options than now. Maybe he knew that USC had more upside given the fertility of their relatively unchallenged recruiting grounds. Maybe being extremely rich in LA is more fun than in OK.

The conventional hindsight analysis that getting rid of a failed leader cannot even be entertained without first securing the successor is a refrain of people who have never been responsible for anything and get to opine without actually having any accountability for outcomes. Yes, I mean journalists. It is vastly preferable to have an elite successor waiting in the wings, but the world does not always cooperate. Retaining bad leadership for "stability" is the province of fools. USC and LSU were well rewarded for wading into the murky depths of the unknown. Florida could not retain a coach who had lost the Swamp. Napier will not do worse than 2-8 over his next ten SEC games, which is how Dan Mullen ended his career. Doubling down on the familiar bad because you fear the unfamiliar unknown is never rewarded. That applies to a lot more than football.

The college football great reset also revealed program hierarchies. Opinions about the best jobs are great and all, but what does the market actually say? Everyone can power rank the best jobs and the lists may look mildly different, but it's rare in college football for a successful head coach to leave the

#9 job for #6. Or #6 for #4. It just doesn't work that way. These are effectively lateral moves. Or so it was once believed. USC and LSU may have more upside potential than Oklahoma and Notre Dame respectively, but established winning coaches just don't jump from one top 10 program to another. Particularly when they are well established and still in good favor. Notre Dame has not had a head coach take another college head coaching job of their own accord since 1907. When was the last time Oklahoma lost a head coach where it wasn't the Sooner athletic director showing them the door? Successful Sooner coaches either leave in scandal (Switzer) or to be network analysts (Bob Stoops, Bud Wilkinson). Not to take another elite college job. Perhaps we are learning about the small differences in hierarchy. Or, at minimum, the willingness of coaches to opportunistically flee what they perceive as a limited upside or proactively dodge a cultural reckoning brewing in their own locker room. Urban Meyer pioneered that art in Florida over a decade ago. Today's coaches don't even have to fake a brain tumor to do it. They can just leave. To say that Notre Dame and Oklahoma were blindsided is an understatement. They should have been. These are uncharted waters. But they are being charted now. No excuse to run up on the shoals anymore. It is right there on the map.

Money also enters into this. Actually, it has already entered, is making itself comfortable on your Barcalounger wearing your slippers and just asked your wife to make dinner. It is central to all of it. Now is when we detail it. Crushing inflation isn't just being felt at the gas pump and the grocery store. Program boosters are having to dig deep. Lincoln Riley is making 100 million over 10 years in South Central and will have an amazing array of benefits. Needless to say, he will not feel a cost of living differential. Brian Kelly will reportedly earn 95 million over 10 years in Baton Rouge. Kelly is currently considering buying the Mississippi river. He was reportedly making just over 5 million per year at Notre Dame. When Texas A&M locked up Jimbo Fisher through 2031 for around 9 million per year, the reactions varied, but laughing at Aggie desperation underpinned much of the analysis. It is always fun, good and right to laugh at Aggies, but they were really showing us the beginning of a shifting set of rules. Unlike Jimbo Fisher, Kelly and Riley were not fleeing a declining program, but the sheer scale of their compensation and length of commitments reconfirm the total transformation of college football markets. The message now is: if you find your guy, lock him up forever. Because someone is coming to money whip 'em.

Before you lock your guy up until he gets social security, caveat emptor. Caveat emptor is not just a cool Latin phrase we can drop so that folks will think we were in Tom Herman's Mensa pledge class. It is an important caution. That lock `em up or lose him argument could have been made on behalf of a successful Dan Mullen in 2020. In fact, Mullen demanded an extension at the end of a three game losing streak and Florida administrators blinked, locking him up through 2026. Where would Florida be if they had locked up Mullen for a full decade in early December of 2020 when the Gators sported a 8-1 record, were ranked #6 in the country, and were highlighted as the hot team no one wanted to face in the postseason? From that program's zenith, Mullen promptly went 5-9 over his next 14 games and 2-8 against SEC opponents. Not good. The Gators' buyout of 12 million dollars was steep, but imagine if that buyout number were 25 million with a decade commitment. Understand that locking up a coach with a decade contract and a massive buyout is not handcuffs on them. It is them handcuffed to you. Are you willing to cut off an arm if things go bad?

Sentimentality and tradition are taking a real beating in this brave new world. Notre Dame is the most storied program in college football history. This is not particularly debatable, even for those who hate the Domers. It is also not that controversial to offer that there are five SEC jobs that are better gigs than South Bend if a coach wishes to position himself for the national title by landing the bluest of blue chips. Those jobs come with expectations, political treachery, and high stakes, but nothing a ten year contract won't remedy. Oklahoma is a far more successful program than USC over the last decade by any objective measure and the school's football commitment is unquestioned. The entire state and school seemingly exist to support the Sooner football program. USC's conference spends more time grappling with microaggressions and how often to test healthy vaccinated 21 year olds for seasonal allergies than figuring out how to reconcile big time athletics to their university missions. California college sports fans are also notorious front runners. But a Trojan program with a profound native recruiting base with almost no local competition is more valuable than a school chock full of loyalists that starts its recruiting focus a three hour drive south and then gets on planes to find the rest of its athletes. It does not hurt that assembling an undefeated season in the Pac 12 looks a lot easier than in Oklahoma's future conference alignment.

Whether an athlete, coach, fan, or administrator, college football is undergoing a profound shift. The warp drive speed of change over the last year has been jarring, almost disorienting, but what has not yet changed is the thrilling expectation of players reporting for summer camp, new faces, old hands, a spirited discussion about the team's prospects, and the hope for a perfect fall day in a packed stadium watching amazing athletes, repping their school and state on the front of their jersey, honoring their family on the back, playing the best game ever invented.

It starts on the offense.

Offensive Overview

The 2021 Texas offense averaged 35.3 points per game and 6.3 yards every time it ran a play. On the surface, those robust numbers are not the typical indicators of a 5-7 football team. While the defense certainly gets blame for the final disappointing season record, the Longhorn offense had more than its share of uneven moments. While explosiveness was not a problem, consistency was. Texas was merely adequate on 3rd down, converting 43.8% of money downs, while scoring touchdowns on 35 of 47 red zone appearances. More tellingly, the offense had a major performance bifurcation in wins and losses. In their five wins, the Horns converted on 58.6% of 3rd downs with a low of 40% against the TCU Horned Frogs. In seven Longhorn losses, the Horns converted only 32.2% of their 3rd downs.

One should expect a difference, but a 26 point differential is more than correlative, it is causative. Even in losses, there were still explosive plays aplenty, but staying on the field was the primary problem. Even when the Longhorns put up 56 points and 574 yards of offense against Kansas while going 7 of 11 on 3rd down, an unimpeachable offensive performance on a surface level, a deeper dive reveals four turnovers, a pick six touchdown, ten penalties, and 24 minutes of ball possession. Yes, the Texas defense was unspeakably soft, but losing to a 2-10 team takes a real team effort. That is why the Texas offense finished the year ranked 35th in the nation by advanced statistics, despite strong top line numbers. That ranking placed Texas just outside of the top quartile of 130 college offenses. Not where Steve Sarkisian wants to be and not where a 2022 team loaded at the skill positions aims to stay.

The 2021 Texas offense had a number of bright spots to build on for 2022 despite a disjointed season performance. Freshman wide receiver Xavier Worthy exploded on the scene and rewrote the freshman Longhorn record book. Bijan Robinson continued his excellence, scoring 15 touchdowns in 10 games. Roschon Johnson led the Longhorns to a win over Kansas State with a get-on-my-back performance in the season finale. Steve Sarkisian showed that he could create big plays in the passing game, whether or not the quarterback hit the open receiver or the offensive line blocked it right and – after Jordan Whittington went down – with a decided absence of real receiving options outside of the true freshman Worthy. With another year of star development, abetted by a talented influx of transfers, Sarkisian's offense will not be on skill position crutches anymore. A healthy Texas (knock on wood) will have the best running back and wide receiver group in the league. That is not bias, that is objective analysis. Beyond the obvious need for better quarterback and offensive line play to enable that skill talent, what are a couple of the big picture subjective elements that might foreshadow season success?

First, the ability to play faster. More specifically, being able to play faster when Texas wants to go fast. The Texas offense played quite slow last year, along with the rest of the Big 12. While the league drew praise for its uncharacteristically gritty defense from the national press, overall scoring also dipped due to a massive decline in total play volume, pace of play, and a malaise in Big 12 quarterbacking quality. Slow offenses score less.

If Texas wants to maximize on offense, which means maximizing the team, they will have to be able to play faster when they need to do so. Due to offensive coordinator changes and better league quarterback play, the rest of the Big 12 is going to play faster next year as well. Does that mean more 59-56 touch football scores from the Big 12 days of old? Maybe. But it will mean that the most successful teams will play at a more varied pace. Playing fast requires quick-minded players knowing what to do in a system that allows for it. Addled brain, slow feet. Typically, playing faster is easier for veteran teams led by experienced quarterbacks with surrounding personnel who are smart enough to understand their duties in varied personnel groupings. It does not require academic genius but it does require football focus, playbook study, and having a player or two on the field who can get the other guys in the right spot. Conditioning also underpins this. How long can Texas go hard at a rapid pace? Endurance in football is about the aggregation of short bursts of maximal intensity. That means strength underlies practical football endurance as much as cardio. Playing fast also relies on staff organization and the cleverness of the offense. A position group that is not well-studied is quickly revealed when timelines shorten and players cannot look to the sideline for a brain transplant. Penalties, lining up wrong, a stupid route, a missed blitz pick up....a head coach can say they want to play fast, but if playing faster means too many mistakes (which slows you down), the coach will throw up his hands and embrace a turtle crawl. One poorly taught position group can hold up an entire offense.

Second, Texas must also play with more flexibility. Texas has more potential for formational diversity than it has had in years. Two running back sets? No problem. Texas has four they like and the best one can run a skinny post from the slot like a wide receiver. Two tight ends? It looks like the Horns may finally have two who can both catch and block. Four wide receivers? Yes, please. Worthy, Neyor, Whittington are a terrific core corps – is it too much to ask to think Texas can develop one more? Formational diversity supported by actual threats creates huge headaches for a defense, but it can also cut the other way. Trying to be all things can mean doing none of them particularly well. It is easier for a classic spread HUNH (hurry-up, no-huddle) team to play fast without errors as there are only a handful of plays to learn and the athletes line up in the same spot every time. Simplicity breeds speed. Running different personnel groups on and off the field – while potentially invaluable and a matchup and assignment nightmare for defenses – raises complexity of execution. Sark must find the balance between hunting mismatches and overwhelming his charges. If he can strike that balance, look out. It is about pushing flexible and fast to the precipice of offensive mistakes, the danger zone where the offense prospers and the defense cannot find their bearings. That requires an on field leader who can put the ball in the right hands: the quarterback.

QUARTERBACK

Player	Height	Weight	Class
Hudson Card	6'2"	199	SO
Quinn Ewers	6'2"	205	FR/RS
Maalik Murphy	6'5"	220	FR/RS
Charles Wright	6'1"	203	FR/RS
Ben Ballard	5'11"	203	JR
Cole Lourd	6'2"	213	FR/RS

	Comp.	Att.	Pct.	Yards	TD	Int	Rating
Hudson Card	51	83	61.4	590	5	1	138.6

Hudson Card had a tumultuous redshirt freshman campaign. Last year, Card was told to get on and off the bench more frequently than a Catholic mass. The splinters in Card's backside were nothing like the splintering of the Longhorn fanbase and media as cults of personality formed around Casey Thompson and, to a lesser degree, Card. It never got to Simms-Applewhite levels in terms of hatred, division, and bizarre fanboy-ism, perhaps because each side eventually had to consider the idea that neither passer was the answer. Will 2022 be another Hail Mary thrown at the quarterback position? An act of faith? Will Texas be led by the Austin native with another year of development or the freshman phenom with hair from a 1982 Loverboy album cover? Whatever the answer, another season of quarterbacking mass musical chairs will see the sacramental wine repurposed into medicinal rather than redemptive use by a Texas fanbase more unforgiving than white pants at a chili cook off.

After drawing a late anointment over Casey Thompson in the season opener, Hudson Card went 14 of 21 for 224 yards and two touchdowns against a plucky 13-1 Ragin Cajun team that featured NFL draft picks in their secondary. The Cajuns, albeit against lesser competition, would go on to rattle off 13 consecutive wins after their defeat in Austin, finishing the year ranked in the Top 20. In that game, Card showed poise and sharp mid-range velocity. It was a promising performance and Texas fans wondered if they had found their next three year starter.

The following week in Fayetteville offered a different perspective.

An overwhelmed Texas offense punted on six of its first seven possessions and was held scoreless in the first half of play. While the putrid play of the offensive line and a puzzling lack of preparation from the Longhorn coaches for the Razorback coverage packages meant plenty of criticism to go around, Card missed open receivers and, more worryingly, showed a breakdown in composure. He was subsequently benched and would not see significant action again until a poor outing against Iowa State and a pick six against Kansas. Card was eventually handed the reins against West Virginia after Sarkisian benched an ineffective Casey Thompson and Texas fans saw glimpses of the signal caller from the season opener. Card showed command, pluck and some much needed deep ball accuracy and would have had an even more impressive box score but for Texas wide receiver drops and bad routes. Just as he found his rhythm, he succumbed to a serious high ankle sprain. Card's season was over. What to make of his season?

Statistically, Card's 2021 season performance was deceptively adequate: he completed 51 of 83 passes for 590 yards at a 61.4% clip, threw five touchdowns with only one interception, and finished with a respectable 138.6 passing efficiency rating. However, a more subjective assessment of his play is less kind than the collective box score. Card's performances in his bookend appearances are beguiling for those interested in counterfactuals. Should the Texas coaches have stuck with their young quarterback to allow him to rebuild confidence after the disaster against Arkansas? If they believed that Card is the player with more tangible upside (and they did), why allow Casey Thompson to start against terrible Rice and Texas Tech defenses, rack up statistics, win over fans, and cement the starting spot? These were potential "get right" games, crucial in the progression of any young passer. Might have playing Card against lesser resistance after his poor performance have righted the ship and sped his trajectory of improvement? Could growth that was evidenced against West Virginia have been realized earlier in the season if the staff had been more patient? A redshirt freshman is supposed to struggle early on the road and the offensive game plan against Arkansas was not faultless. Or was it as simple as the staff watching the film against Arkansas, realizing that Card was not seeing the field, and that the only viable option for their credibility with the team was trying another hand? Perhaps the team was flat in part because of Card's lack of command. As with all counterfactuals, we will never know. The hard truth is that Hudson offered plenty of evidence for his detractors. But that was last year. The rearview mirror is considerably smaller than the windshield for a reason. So let us assess the road ahead.

Now in his third program year, Hudson Card brings lanky athleticism (he has a 36 inch vertical leap) and a zippy release to the starting quarterback battle. Card is most comfortable in hurry-up spread formations resembling his Lake Travis roots when Texas plays fast and he can get the ball out quickly to a pre snap identification. Clean reads, pace, and rhythm are his friends. Muddier windows can paralyze him, he loses decisiveness, and his accuracy takes a dive, particularly when throwing deep balls outside of the hashes. However, Card in rhythm, making quick decisions, and getting the ball out fast can look like a million bucks. Velocity, ball placement in tight windows, it is all there. But progressing through the second and third read from play action? Or hitting the set piece "gotcha" play downfield that Sark has been setting up all game? Card has a lot to prove.

If Hudson Card's ability to earn the reins of the offense will be predicated on his ability to hit the big plays exploiting a particular defensive tendency that Steve Sarkisian draws up three or four times per game, Quinn Ewers' ability to earn the starting nod will be predicated on his ability to make the mundane throws and pre snap adjustments necessary for consistent offense and avoiding too many gunslinging errors.

Quinn Ewers is a former five star high school phenom and one of the highest ranked quarterback recruits in Texas history. Ewers was a unique pure passing talent at Southlake Carroll where, as early as his sophomore year, he showed terrific feel, varied ball placement on tough throws, and underrated athleticism. He also showed the knack for releasing the ball accurately from a dizzying variety of arm angles. His journey to Texas is the sort of weird ride that could only happen in the new world of paid amateurism and portal hopping. Ewers chose to skip his senior season of high school for Ohio State and a reported 1.4 million dollars in NIL money endorsing, among other things, kombucha. He regretted that decision (perhaps he prefers fermented kefir) and transferred from Columbus to Austin, so he is still technically a freshman. That irregular start to his career raises legitimate concern about what makes the young man tick, but those concerns were allayed when Ewers arrived in Austin and demonstrated a humble demeanor and dedication to his craft.

Can the talented freshman passer overcome peroxide poisoning from his glorious dyed blonde mullet and a weird beginning to his career to win the Longhorn starting job decisively? Whilst possibly also earning a Supercuts endorsement? Yes. As the spring game evidenced, Ewers has a lot to offer. Quinn Ewers looked like an inexperienced, talented quarterback with natural instincts and the ability to fit in nearly every throw that Brett Favre ever invented. Whether a deep post dime to Isaiah Neyor or a flawless RPO in the red zone to Xavier Worthy. He also threw several other quality balls where the receiver did not complete the play. Ewers is a talented thrower with a diverse menu of touch and ball placement.

Of course, we talkin' bout practice. Games are their own animal and freshman saviors at the quarterback position have a generally unsatisfying history. However, it would be foolish to underestimate how beguiling Ewers' skill set is to a great offensive mind. Sark understands that he would have to pare down the offense into bite sized chunks, but the options available in those chunks means a defense that must defend the entire field and the potential to unlock a group of skill players that could dominate the Big 12. Ewers has demonstrated preternatural feel, timing, and small window accuracy, with an arm that can threaten every section of the field. *In practice.* Could Ewers be the catalyst that Sark needs to make his offense truly multidimensional, where every defensive choice is the wrong answer? Or should Texas take the more judicious and responsible approach and let the freshman grow into his powers on a more conservative timeline? One thing is clear about Ewers. He has a trait that fans favor above all others: no track record. A blank slate, where any outcome can be imagined. Fans like to take that blank slate and fill in the literary genius of William Faulkner and Joseph Conrad, when reality is more often Fifty Shades of Gray.

Charles Wright is a redshirt freshman fighting for the 3rd spot in the depth chart. Wright showed a live arm in high school at Austin High a few miles from the Longhorn campus, but limited action in open practice environments shows that he has a ways to go.

The imposing Maalik Murphy looks like a 5th year college quarterback, but the young signal caller from California is still raw and unrefined and will be a longer term project. Despite spending the spring recovering from a leg injury, Murphy impressed coaches with his attitude, work ethic, and unselfishness.

Prognosis

The 2022 spring game settled the University of Texas quarterback controversy decisively in that it is still decisively unsettled. Hudson Card demonstrated clear growth from a decidedly uneven 2021 and Quinn Ewers showed glimpses of NFL level ball placement. From a growth standpoint, Card was particularly sharp in a hurry-up, throw-to-the-pre-snap-read offense while Ewers threw a "What are you looking at?" interception to Anthony Cook.

However, in assessing this battle, indecision may be a feature, not a bug. The hard reality is that Texas needs two viable starting level quarterbacks in order to fulfill its ambitions of a Big 12 championship and to initiate a turnaround from a decade plus long program malaise. Football is a violent sport and losing a starting quarterback or having one sufficiently injured that they cannot play well is not really bad luck. It's more or less probable. Particularly with a potentially incomplete offensive line that will need to grow into its best upside and given the injury history of the two primary quarterback candidates. The loss of a quarterback is also felt more profoundly on an offensive-oriented team that may struggle early on defense and lacks the supportive infrastructure of a senior-laden offensive line that can run the ball 50 times a game and protect a backup. No, Texas needs a viable back-up quarterback who can throw the ball around and put up points.

An established, loaded program is better inoculated to losing a signal caller. That loaded team may not fulfill their ultimate goals if their preferred signal caller goes down, but the wheels won't come off. Conversely, a program trying to break out from 5-7 has little margin for error. Texas fans lived in that margin of error last year with injuries to both Hudson Card and Casey Thompson. The Texas offensive line must still prove its mettle and Steve Sarkisian is not schematically averse to giving up a shot on his quarterback in exchange for an open receiver downfield. While the coaches must respect the sacred nature of meritocratic competition at the most visible and important position, they also must confront the reality that naming a starter now could create a depth vacuum that might threaten to suck the entire season's upside down the drain. The portal is always whispering in the ear of the disaffected.

3rd string quarterback Charles Wright is not yet ready for game action, though that might change with substantial progress in August camp. Freshman Maalik Murphy has drawn early praise as a potential program guy and a dedicated athlete, but he needs years of development to be a potentially viable starter. Cole Lourd and Ben Ballard are several cuts above the average walk-on, but they are walk-ons for a reason. The drop off from the Card/Ewers option is precipitous. Without a viable second option, Texas is virtually guaranteed a disappointing season and Sarkisian's pitch for long term progress gets tougher to swallow for recruits and fans alike.

So how to keep both options?

Last year, peculiar rotations and personnel groupings in practice and the spring game suggested that Steve Sarkisian was interested in keeping both Casey Thompson and Hudson Card engaged in the starting quarterback battle until the opening game of the season. If he saw a clear hierarchy in the candidates, he certainly did not want them perceiving it. While Sarkisian's reluctance to name a starter until late may have reflected the close nature of the contest, that idea does not also preclude the staff from placing the occasional finger lightly on the scales to ensure that two viable quarterbacks were available when the season started. If that sounds Machiavellian, welcome to big time college football.

Steve Sarkisian boasts a well-deserved reputation as a QB guru and he has coached a variety of throwers to elite success at the college and NFL level. He has also managed to inflate several NFL draft values along the way, generally by featuring the very best attributes of his signal callers and minimizing their weaknesses. Matt Sanchez loves Steve Sarkisian as much as the New York Jets curse him. No player Sark starts will be without weaknesses. The question is: which weaknesses will be easiest to scheme around? Which weaknesses are most likely to be a drag on a supporting cast of good to elite skill position players? The starting nod will go to the quarterback whose deficiencies can best be masked, who can distribute the ball accurately and on time to talented runners and receivers. The starter will be the athlete who can be a conduit of offense, rather than its wellspring. Don't expect a starting quarterback to be named anytime soon. Or anytime before a week out from Louisiana-Monroe. Whether because of a truly competitive race, realpolitik roster management, or a dash of both.

RUNNING BACK

Player	Height	Weight	Class
Bijan Robinson	6'0"	221	JR
Roschon Johnson	6'2"	219	SR
Keilan Robinson	5'9"	183	JR
Jonathon Brooks	6'0"	205	FR/RS
Jaydon Blue	6'0"	194	FR

	Rushing				Receiving			
	Att	Yds	Avg	TD	Rec	Yds	Avg	TD
Bijan Robinson	195	1127	5.8	11	26	295	11.3	4
Roschon Johnson	96	577	5.9	5	11	83	7.5	0
Keilan Robinson	45	333	7.2	3	7	57	8.1	0
Jonathan Brooks	21	143	6.8	1	1	12	12	0

Bijan Robinson is a special runner with the potential to be an all-timer at a school that has had more than its share of all-timer running backs. Despite his 215+ pound frame, Robinson has the cutting ability of a scatback forty pounds lighter, but he also runs with power and purpose when the hard yards are needed. As a sophomore, he compiled 1127 yards rushing at 5.8 yards per carry with 11 touchdowns.

He also added 26 receptions for 295 yards and 4 touchdowns as a pass catcher. Impressive numbers despite missing two games with an injury. Robinson particularly excels in the outside zone running game, lulling defenders with a lateral flow to the sideline, interrupting the sideline sprint with a ankle-breaking cut up the field if he sees green, or a dash around the corner if the exterior blockers wash down the edge defenders. While Texas will not run a great deal of classic outside zone, Robinson's attributes translate nicely to any running scheme.

While Robinson gets up to speed incredibly quickly, he lacks a top gear and can be run down. He can also improve as a pass protector. However, given his receiving ability, you may not want him blocking too much. Bijan is a very good receiver out of the backfield, demonstrating soft hands and a good feel for the screen game. He is also fully capable of splitting out and running real routes. If he dedicated the time to the position, he could easily be a starting wide receiver. For that reason, when the matchups find him up against a linebacker, get ready for the fight song. Aside from his unique combination of size with single cut explosiveness, Bijan has elite level vision and a terrific feel for how to set up defenders. A sterling citizen off of the field and a tireless worker, Bijan is a terrific role model for his teammates and the program. Over two years, Robinson has compiled 2,321 combined rushing and receiving yards from scrimmage and, if he remains healthy, it is a good bet that he will add considerably to that tally in 2022.

Roschon Johnson is one of the most beloved players in the Texas program for his unselfishness, team-first attitude, leadership by example, and toughness.

Over three years, the former dual threat quarterback has compiled 1636 yards rushing (at 5.5 yards per carry) and scored 20 total touchdowns to go with 42 catches.

A highly capable runner, blocker, and receiver, the multifaceted Johnson willed the Longhorns to a win in the final game of the season against Kansas State playing running back and wildcat quarterback, amassing 179 yards on a season high 31 carries. Though the 225 pound runner is not blessed with any single outstanding attribute, he has no real weaknesses. He's a terrific complement to Bijan Robinson and a rock solid part of a very talented running back rotation. Johnson is a terrific team leader by example, but the Longhorn coaches need him to be more vocal.

Keilan Robinson transferred to the 40 Acres from Alabama and the DC area athlete brought a special level of quickness, which he evidenced as a runner and as the premier punt blocker in the conference.

Robinson is an unselfish member of a crowded and talented running back room and his willingness to star on special teams as a kick blocking specialist highlights the sort of team-first attitude that must permeate the entire program. Of course, Robinson is also damn good at his primary job: running the football. He totaled 322 yards and 3 touchdowns on 45 carries for an impressive 7.2 yards per carry average, including a strong 9 carry, 111 yard performance at West Virginia. The 185 pound junior is a talented scatback, but he would greatly improve his versatility, playing time, and future chances of playing at the next level if he was a more credible passing game threat, not only from the backfield, but from the slot.

Jonathon Brooks hates being tackled as much as spell check hates his first name. He turned heads in limited action last year with his deceptive running style. He had 143 yards on 21 carries and one touchdown, proving that the Longhorn running back room talent is both deep and wide.

Jaydon Blue should redshirt.

Prognosis

Texas has one of the best running back rooms in the country. Bijan Robinson is a 1st round NFL talent with terrific versatility as a runner and receiver. Roschon Johnson and Keilan Robinson would start at half of the FBS schools in America. You know a room is good when Texas fans rave about the 4th string runner Jonathon Brooks like he's an indie rock band. "Sure, everyone loves Bijan, but he is so commercial and well known. Brooks runs so authentically. I discovered him first. You should see him without pads, unplugged." New running back coach Tashard Choice has limitless options with this group and you can bet that the Longhorns will incorporate two running back personnel sets to hunt matchups and get some of their best, most explosive, and reliable players on the field. While it is tempting to feed a talent like Bijan Robinson 30 touches a game, the quality behind him means that Texas has the option of preserving the talented Arizona native, keeping his legs fresh, and attacking opponents with a variety of athletes and running styles. Keep an eye on potential passing game opportunities for this group. If the wide receiver and tight end groups prove to be as good as hoped for, there is going to be a lot of underneath space available for Robinson, Johnson and Robinson to exploit.

WIDE RECEIVER

Player	Height	Weight	Class
Xavier Worthy	6'1"	163	SO
Jordan Whittington	6'1"	209	JR
Isaiah Neyor	6'3"	218	JR
Troy Omeire	6'3"	221	SO
Agiye Hall	6'3"	195	SO
Tarique Milton	5'10"	195	SR
Jaden Alexis	6'0"	189	FR/RS
Casey Cain	6'2"	195	FR/RS
Savion Red	5'10"	210	FR

	Receiving				Rushing			
	Rec	Yds	Avg	TD	Att	Yds	Avg	TD
Xavier Worthy	62	981	15.8	12	1	7	7	0
Jordan Whittington	26	377	14.5	3	1	8	8	0
Isaiah Neyor	44	878	20	12	12	23	1.9	1
Agiye Hall	4	72	18	2				
Tarique Milton	15	278	18.5	3				

Xavier Worthy, one time Michigan commitment, abandoned Ann Arbor for Austin and Texas coaches and fans are delighted that he did. The skinny sophomore speed merchant from Fresno showed grit, tenacity, elite quickness, and frequent dominance during his freshman campaign for the Longhorns. Along the way, Worthy earned 1st Team All-Big 12 honors and set Longhorn freshmen receiving records for receptions (62), yardage (981), and touchdowns (12).

A phenomenal 9 catch, 261 yard performance against Oklahoma highlighted his big game competitiveness and love of the spotlight while a late game kickoff return fumble from deep in the Longhorn end zone also demonstrated the dangers of a true freshman who believes he can make every play. The problem in convincing Worthy otherwise is that he is usually right. If Xavier can add a touch of wisdom and experience to his considerable athletic traits and drive, Worthy could be the most dangerous receiver in college football. A review of the season suggests that Worthy's upside was capped more by surrounding talent than hitting the freshman wall and it is interesting to consider that the upgrade in skill talent around him may yield Worthy even more opportunities and game impact. The rail thin 165 pound Worthy is surprisingly durable and is as good after the catch as he is threatening a corner deep. A solid route runner for his age, further advancements there could make him virtually unstoppable without bracket coverage. While Worthy is also a terrific potential weapon on punt and kickoff returns, the Texas coaches may choose to preserve the slightly built speedster from the threat of injury. Discretion is the better part of valor and a healthy Worthy is the best part of what could be a profligate deep ball Longhorn passing offense. Worthy is one of the premier receivers in the country and the centerpiece for what should be the best receiving corps in the Big 12 conference.

A classic overlooked dark horse recruit, Arlington native **Isaiah Neyor** came to football late in life, bloomed even later than that, and then saw his prepster recruiting evaluations handicapped by COVID disruptions. Neyor went to Wyoming where the big wide out earned All-Conference honors in his second season, catching 44 balls for 878 yards and 12 touchdowns. Despite poor Cowboy quarterback play, it is notable that Neyor caught eight touchdowns over his last six games and that he accounted for 41.5% of Wyoming's passing offense overall.

For comparison's sake, Xavier Worthy was the solitary meaningful threat in the 2021 Longhorn passing attack and he accounted for 36.3% of the Horn passing offense. Neyor's trademark is deceptive change-of-pace and the ability to win balls downfield with a terrific catch radius, sticky hands, and good adjustments to the football. He is a tracker, not a blazer, but accurate ball radar and the ability to win a ball in tight spaces is one of the most important, least appreciated aspects of productive wide receiver play. How will he handle the level up in competition from the Mountain West to the Big 12? The current outlook is optimistic. Ever since arriving on campus, Neyor has impressed with better than anticipated athleticism, better size (this was mentioned by every source), and a wider skill set than was first perceived. The spring game highlighted Neyor's athleticism, willingness to block (crucial for fully unleashing Worthy's screen game and Bijan outside) and Neyor is about the same size as some members of the Longhorn tight end room. An offseason injury setback to one of his hands should be cleared up by August. So how will Isaiah Neyor adapt to the Big 12? The better question might be: how is the Big 12 going to adapt to Neyor?

Jordan Whittington can catch the ball, but he can't catch a break. The talented Cuero product has seen an unending succession of injuries upend his developmental trajectory during his time at Texas. In his freshman year, he only played in one game before succumbing to injury. In his sophomore year, he managed only five. Last year, he managed eight games, returning after a four game absence that saw the Longhorn passing game denuded and without options to complement Worthy. Based upon that mathematical progression of game participation, Texas can project double digit starts in 2022. Science, ladies and gentlemen.

Whittington totaled 26 catches for 377 yards and 3 touchdowns last year, with his season high performance against Louisiana in the opener, but the next week was his season low water mark against Arkansas, where he uncharacteristically dropped a pair of catchable balls. Whittington is in the big slot mold – not necessarily height, but mass – who gets open with first step quickness and body control despite his 210 pound frame. Whittington looked terrific in the spring game, reminding everyone how difficult he is to get on the turf after the catch. A healthy Whittington is a fine complement to Neyor and Worthy, fully capable of punishing a defense for overplaying dynamic outside threats, in addition to being a potential chain mover behind the linebackers and in front of the safeties. Jordan's health is key and the lack of other viable options at slot receiver means that Whittington is more important to Longhorn offensive upside than some may assume.

Tarique Milton is a late portal addition from Iowa State where the 5th year senior amassed 1519 yards on 99 catches and 7 touchdowns over his career. He did most of his damage early in his career as a freshman and sophomore (722 yards at over 20 yards per catch in his sophomore year), but multiple injury woes sidelined his career and degraded his athleticism. Whether that athletic ability can regenerate is unknown. Texas coaches will find out soon enough. At minimum, Milton is a savvy veteran who will bring much needed depth, experience, and consistency to an offense that sorely needs quality back ups and reliable receivers who can run right to the right spot and make the catch when Worthy, Whittington, and Neyor draw the lion's share of coverage attention. There are free yards available to a smart, competent receiver when Texas goes four wide. One who can read a defense, run to open space, and catch the ball. That does not sound terribly hard, but there is a reason coaches love reliable role players.

Complementing Milton's potentially steady veteran presence is a much more dynamic, perhaps even volatile, athlete: **Agiye Hall**. Hall represents pure unbridled upside, but unlike Milton, he has not earned plaudits for his off-field focus and steady presence. A former elite recruit (he was a 2021 Top 50 national player) and a potential NFL level talent (Hall is 6'3" and ran a 4.5 40 with a 37 inch vertical leap as a high school senior), Hall was invited to leave Alabama for a perceived lack of program commitment and general unreliability. In the national title game against Georgia, Hall replaced an injured

Jameson Williams and showed his ability with two catches for 52 yards, but he also had a couple of crucial drops and blew some route reads. Hall has the opportunity for a fresh start in Austin and if the offensive staff can carve out a role for a fully bought in Agiye – even a simple three route combination – he could be a dangerous weapon, even at 20-25 snaps per game. If it goes the other way, Hall could contribute some sideline pouts and a transfer. Either way, the Horns are playing with house money.

Jaden Alexis missed the spring game due to an injury, but the Florida product, son of former NFL runner Rich Alexis, has earned some positive reviews based on his informal workouts. The Texas coaching staff would welcome Jaden becoming a reliable backup on a receiving corps that has very good front line talent and zero proven depth.

Troy Omeire has been hamstrung by a pair of knee injuries, limiting the dynamic 6-3, 225 pound receiver and preventing him from showing what he can do in games after drawing raves as a true freshman in August camp. Observers gushed about his hands, physicality, catch radius, route running, and surprising explosiveness. There are questions about whether multiple knee injuries have substantially degraded his athleticism, but if Omeire can return to form, the receiving depth chart will be considerably better.

Casey Cain was a lightly recruited prospect from Louisiana but the lean wideout has worked his way up the depth chart and should participate in the Longhorn wide receiver rotation. While Cain lacks explosive speed or dynamism, he is a smooth route runner with long arms.

Brenen Thompson can absolutely fly (10.24 100 meter times are always welcome) and that speed will certainly see the field as a freshman. Getting elite speed on a defense's second tier coverage guys may merit a Sark whiteboard session or two. **Savion Red** will start his career at wide receiver. Expect a redshirt.

Prognosis

Texas will have the best starting receivers in the Big 12 and should boast a top ten unit nationally. However, there is a major drop off in reliability from the starters to the second and third team units. Health will be a major factor in the troika of Worthy, Neyor and Whittington dominating at the level of their potential, as will be the development of solid complementary options to backstop the aforementioned. The potential is certainly there for the entire group to blossom into something special, but transfers like Tarique Milton and Agiye Hall, as well as youngsters like Brenen Thompson, Jaden

Alexis and Casey Cain, must perform. Troy Omeire's ability to contribute meaningfully will be determined in August camp. Even a diminished Omeire can be a valuable role player simply by virtue of his frame and hands. This is the most talented bunch of wide receivers at Texas since Jordan Shipley and Quan Cosby (with supporting cast shout outs to Kirkendoll, Collins, Williams) worked over the 2008 schedule every Saturday. Notably, Shipley and Cosby were maximizers and overachievers who could read coverages like pros. If this current crew can even approach that level of commitment and understanding of the game, look out. The baseline talent level is as good as it's been at Texas in well over a decade. Can the offense unlock it?

After an offseason purge of the Longhorn wide receiver room, the Longhorn staff has sensibly cut the scholarship numbers at the position so that the Horns no longer carry a needless excess of wide receivers. Under Brennan Marion, Texas is now recruiting and developing narrowly, tailored to fit. Wide receiver recruiting is no longer flinging random bodies at the position and hoping for a better outcome. This is basic competent roster management in total team scholarship allocation. It also allowed the house money transfers of Milton and Hall and frees up practice repetitions and more individual teaching time across the board. Given how frequently the state of Texas high school ranks churns out quality wide receivers and the wide availability of wide receivers in the portal, why get a bunch and store them on your roster? Let others store them and go shopping when you need them. Why are you filling up your garage with paper towels from Costco? Let them store it for you and pick `em up as needed. Crucially, a lean wide receiver room also clarifies roles and hierarchies. That is imperative for unit and team chemistry and fosters fewer complaints from a position group that can put the prima into primadona and will scramble the letters in t-e-a-m until they get m-e. With only one ball to nourish the hungry, streamlining the mouths to feed and removing false depth means more calories for everyone. Now, it is Marion and Sark's job to choose who eats first.

TIGHT END

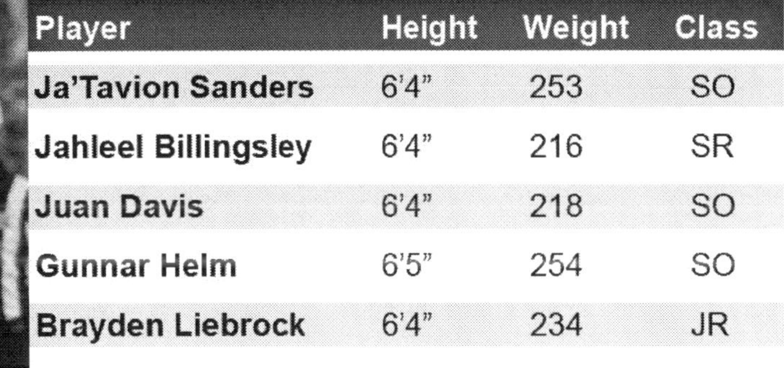

Player	Height	Weight	Class
Ja'Tavion Sanders	6'4"	253	SO
Jahleel Billingsley	6'4"	216	SR
Juan Davis	6'4"	218	SO
Gunnar Helm	6'5"	254	SO
Brayden Liebrock	6'4"	234	JR

	Receiving				Rushing			
	Rec	Yds	Avg	TD	Att	Yds	Avg	TD
Juan Davis	1	0	0	0				
Jahleel Billingsley	17	256	15.1	3				

Ja'Tavion Sanders is the most talented tight end at Texas since Jermichael Finley. That is a bold, perhaps reckless, comparison for a player that has not yet caught a pass in live action, but the talent, skill, size and ability are all there. All he needs are the repetitions and to learn the hard lessons a player only learns in games. In the spring game, Sanders revealed himself to be a competent blocker in all phases: pass blocking, run blocking with a hand down, flexed out in space, and finally, lead blocking through the hole as a classic H-back.

That was a pleasant surprise for a player perceived as a receiving tight end and if it translates to game action, Texas will have a chess piece on the board that it has not had in years. Throw in his natural receiving ability with hands, size, and fluidity and Texas has a real underneath complement to an exciting wide receiving corps. Sanders is not from the raw freak phylum of tight ends – like Gronk, Vernon Davis – rather his athleticism is more subtle: body control, ease of lateral movement, coordination, wingspan. Sanders is an easy mover and those guys tend to have a knack for finding themselves open, irrespective of their straight line 40 times. Inexperience means that it will take some time and game reps for it to all come together, but Sanders will be a NFL prospect by his junior season.

Gunnar Helm has also developed nicely and quietly worked his way up the depth chart over more hyped companions. The big Coloradan is a better pass catcher and pure blocker than he is perceived and he possesses good feet for a 6-5, 255 pound athlete. Helm was a nice out of state find and as he grows into his body, the former high school flex tight end will continue to improve as a blocker and further cement himself as the second most complete tight end on the roster.

Jahleel Bllingsley transferred to Texas from Alabama and the former Tide tight end grabbed 37 balls for 559 yards and six touchdowns over his career in Tuscaloosa. A career where Jahleel seemingly spent as much time in Nick Saban's doghouse as his dorm room.

Billingsley is a pure flex or receiving tight end and has consistently carried between 215-225 pounds over his career, demurring on gaining the weight that Alabama encouraged him to add to his frame. Billingsley is a good athlete and has the fan thirsty stamp of Alabama lineage, but while he will invariably play a role in the 2022 offense, Ja'Tavion Sanders is the more complete player and when Texas goes with two tight ends to power the run and play action game, it is a good bet that Sarkisian will opt for a solid blocker with some receiving ability over a solid receiver with little blocking ability. When Alabama needed secondary pass catchers to step up in the national title game with their top two pass receivers absent with injury, Billingsley did not dent the box score. Meanwhile, starting tight end Cameron Latu, who beat out Billingsley for the starting job earlier in the year, had 5 catches for 102 yards in that contest. Billingsley has actually lost more weight since that game, checking in during the spring at 215 pounds. If you want to further complicate the arrows on the depth chart, consider that Jordan Whittington's true backup in the slot, in the absence of a wide receiver stepping up, might just be a flexed out Billingsley.

Juan Davis has Juan in a million versatility as a former all-district quarterback in high school, but he is on the longer term development plan at tight end. Davis currently tops out around 220 pounds and is unlikely to be an effective in-line blocker, but he is rugged, does not mind mixing it up, and is a fairly nifty pass catcher in the short game.

Brayden Liebrock has missed too much practice and development time with injuries to reasonably project his impact. Until the junior can demonstrate more consistent health, his career is a black box. Durability is an ability and right now that is Liebrock's biggest question mark. All of that written, despite Brayden's inability to stay healthy, it should be noted that the coaches have not yet encouraged him to seek other options. There is a reason they are waiting to see a healthy Liebrock this August and it is all about his potential.

Prognosis

The Texas tight end room has more talent and potentially well-rounded skill sets than it has seen in a while. What the room sorely lacks is game experience. While many Longhorn fans expected Jahleel Billingsley to have the inside track at starting due to his experience and seeing him play in big games at Bama, that is likely not in the cards for the type of offense that Steve Sarkisian wants to run. Sark prefers well rounded, versatile tight ends over specialists. The best current embodiments of that ideal are Ja'Tavion Sanders and Gunnar Helm, in that order. Billingsley can play a very useful, narrower role, and might see that role expanded with injuries, but he lacks diversity of use. If you are looking for a totally unexpected wildcard contributor, a healthy Braden Liebrock will have a chance to live up to his recruiting billing this August.

OFFENSIVE LINE

Player	Height	Weight	Class
Christian Jones	6'6"	313	SR
Hayden Conner	6'5"	320	SO
Junior Angilau	6'6"	316	SR
Jake Majors	6'3"	313	SO
Andrej Karic	6'4"	297	SO
Cole Hutson	6'5"	309	FR
Jaylen Garth	6'5"	297	SO
Sawyer Goram-Welch	6'4"	306	SO
Isaiah Hookfin	6'5"	281	JR
Logan Parr	6'4"	315	FR/RS
Max Merril	6'4"	299	FR/RS
Michael Balis	6'5"	288	JR
Chad Wolf	6'3"	261	JR
Devon Campbell	6'3"	310	FR
Kelvin Banks	6'5"	300	FR
Neto Umeozulu	6'4"	285	FR
Malik Agbo	6'5"	320	FR
Cameron Williams	6'5"	360	FR
Conner Robertson	6'4"	296	FR

Christian Jones' career has been an exercise in patience. Patience from the coaches and the fanbase for his failings as a pass protector and more patience from Christian to trust his size and athleticism against edge defenders and stop beating himself mentally by abandoning fundamentals when things start to spiral.

Jones has earned 22 starts and 35 appearances in his time at Texas and it is time for the senior to take the next step. Jones is a fine athlete who carries 315 pounds on a 6-6 frame about as well as an offensive tackle can, but he lacks consistent technique and when he starts to struggle against a pass rusher, he reverts to bad habits rather than falling back to his base of training. In fairness to Jones, he has had multiple offensive line coaches and has likely been taught multiple inconsistent techniques, but it is time he picked one he likes. The move to right tackle from left is a positive and he seems more comfortable on that side. Some tackles have a dominant side. Time will reveal whether that is true for Jones. Despite his pass blocking woes, Jones can be a good, sometimes devastating, run blocker. Remember that Jones did not play football until his junior year of high school, preferring soccer. Jones' senior season at Texas could find him starting at right tackle, as first tackle off of the bench, or even a starting guard. The smart money says starting right tackle, but smart and dumb money alike have no idea if Jones will plateau or see the light turn on his final season.

It was not long ago that a true freshman center was pressed into emergency duty at the end of the 2020 season, where he performed well enough to get the head start on a starting job in 2021. Sophomore **Jake Majors** has already started 14 games as a Longhorn and the Academic 1st Team All-Big 12 selection has plenty of good ball ahead of him.

Majors has a unique ability to cut off nose tackles with deft footwork and open up cutback lanes for Bijan Robinson and Roschon Johnson while also creating a choke point for backside pursuit. Majors is not particularly powerful at the point of contact, but he has active feet and he defeats defensive linemen by getting to a spot first and then washing out the defender if they overcommit. Majors can struggle to hold up against massive nose tackles on interior run plays, but another year of physical development should help him. Having a reliable center to coordinate line calls will be key for a potentially young Texas offensive line, not to mention the possibility of helping to identify protections for a freshman quarterback. Major is a fine stabilizing piece for the Texas line. Do not be surprised if he leaves Austin having started over 50 games, finally promoted to Jake Generals. Yes, this preview gets one Dad joke.

Junior Angilau is a 5th year guard with 34 career starts under his belt. Now the graybeard of the offensive line, Angilau will be counted on for leadership, consistency, and communication as Kyle Flood integrates a host of talented young freshmen and sophomores and tries to find better consistency from his veterans.

Angilau is built long for a guard and despite his height, he demonstrates excellent punch at the point of attack when he keeps his pads down and feet driving. Junior has struggled in pass protection against stunting defensive lines and heavy interior blitzing, but against physical, power-oriented defensive lines, Angilau has been frequently outstanding. He played particularly well in the 2019 Alamo Bowl against a physical Utah defensive line packed with NFL draft picks. Angilau is stereotyped as a mauler, but film review reveals that he is a capable blocker on the move with better than average athleticism. His pass protection has exhibited maddening holes, sometimes allowing a rusher to run right past him without contact, but one must wonder where individual confusion ends and poor unit coordination begins. Either way, Kyle Flood badly needs his veterans to step up and lead.

Andrej Karic has played in fourteen games with two starts in his Longhorn career. He demonstrates good feet, a live motor, and outstanding technique blocking outside zone in the running game, but he has struggled mightily at times in pass protection. As a pass defender, Karic typically uses his feet well, but he lacks ideal arm length and longer defenders can slap down his arms before he can get extension and they get into his pads, at which point Karic is at a disadvantage. Karic's feet and aggression translate well to guard and center, but the coaches have not yet tried him there. Karic missed the spring game due to injury, but should be fully recovered by August camp. Any 2022 outcome is possible for Karic – including starting left tackle in the opener against Lousiana-Monroe – but at minimum he will be a key utility asset. His athleticism and motor are rare assets and he has the tools to excel in certain schemes, but he may not fit Kyle Flood's size-infatuated preferences.

Hayden Conner fits Flood's size requirements nicely. In fact, he fits the size requirements for the antagonist in a Godzilla movie. Hayden saw game action last year in eight contests and impressed in limited snaps, but he was the talk of spring camp due to his improvement and demonstrated versatility. The coaches feel increasingly comfortable starting Conner at tackle or guard, though his best money position down the road will probably be on the inside. Conner's primary assets are his aggression, attention to detail, and ability to stay on blocks. While 6-5, 320 is not uncommon in a college offensive lineman, not all big guys are created equally in how they wear that weight. Conner wears it well but he also wears it big. He also has a bully mentality between the lines. A trait that has been sorely missing from Texas offensive lines for some time. Evidenced every time someone cheap shots a Texas quarterback and the offensive line mills around watching instead of trying to make that defender wear their helmet inside their body.

Given his ability to move mass around the field, it is unsurprising that Conner is a Physics major and the Longhorns need more bodies up front that tend to stay in motion rather than at rest. While totally unproven as a starter, some in the program believe that Conner is the best guard on the team and, given enough practice time to develop, could be the best tackle. So where to start him? Where he best helps the team. If the tackles are adequate, he will start at guard. If a tackle is less than adequate, the coaches will likely ask Conner to adapt outside. Hayden Conner is starting in 2022. Where he starts depends on what hole Flood feels he most needs to fill.

Cole Hutson was the sole early enrollee for the much hyped 2022 offensive line class. Hutson was less heralded than several of his peers, but he had a fantastic spring that culminated in a very capable performance in the spring game. If Hutson was supposed to be the high floor program guy that the coaches bring along slowly, the physical young guard from Frisco did not get that memo. He is some time away from starting, but Hutson is exceeding early expectations.

Logan Parr is entering his third year at Texas and has seen action in four games. He was adequate in the spring game, but he will need to fend off some impressive new blood if he wants to earn a potential starting job in 2023 or 2024.

Sawyer Gorham-Welch was moved from a packed defensive line room to guard this offseason. Despite his reservations, it was the best possible move for Gorham-Welch's future development. As a general rule, even average defensive line athleticism will make that player one of the more athletic offensive linemen on the team. If Gorham-Welch is committed to succeed and can pick up the finer points of offensive line play, these conversions can work out with real upside.

Isaiah Hookfin was generating a lot of positive buzz before a serious motorcycle accident in late 2021. Hookfin broke eight ribs, his forearm, his collarbone, and lacerated his spleen. He missed development time, lost a lot of weight, and will spend 2022 on medical scholarship.

Jaylen Garth suffered serious knee injuries before enrolling at Texas that seriously degraded his mobility and development. In the spring game, he showed aggression as a run blocker, but he struggled badly as a pass protector. Garth is a long term project who will have to defend his depth chart status from a pack of hungry freshmen wolves.

Max Merril needs seasoning and a lot of time in the weight room.

Devon Campbell, **Kelvin Banks**, **Cam Williams**, **Neto Umeozulu**, **Malik Ogbo** and **Connor Robertson (Cole Hutson discussed above)** form the most heralded offensive line class in Longhorn history. Though none of them joined classmate Cole Hutson as an early enrollee, many expect this bunch to compete for depth chart spots early, to include contesting for starting jobs at tackle and guard. Devon Campbell and Kelvin Banks are the most likely candidates to do so, but please see the recruiting section of this preview for a full rundown of their various attributes.

Prognosis

Christian Jones, Jake Majors and Junior Angilau have 70 combined starts over their careers. That's not a bad start for forming the core of any offensive line group, but there is a chance that Jones could be beaten out at right tackle (or conversely, have the light turn on and blossom into a All-Big 12 status, as butterflies land on our fingers and birds break into song) and there is little doubt that youngsters like sophomore Hayden Conner and the true freshmen class will play a prominent role on the depth chart. Counting on freshmen offensive linemen to reliably fill out a depth chart is more perilous than streaking a rattlesnake roundup, but this incoming freshman offensive line class is truly gifted. This preview has observed Classes of Beef before. Texas does this offensive line Class of Beef thing about every 5-7 years. Lots of hype, they enroll, decimate local Austin buffets, jam up the plumbing in the Gregory dorms, and most of them disappoint. It is a marketing line meant to peddle hope. A description of volume, not quality. That is not the case with this 2022 group, even though all developmental caveats for the offensive line position certainly apply. They have to want it and the S&C and offensive line coaching must be on point.

Asking that level of talent to round out the two deep is not a tall order. Asking one or two of them to become starters at some point during the season may be, but it is not entirely crazy. It is also possible that the on campus veterans could form a decent enough starting unit that Flood will not be forced to start freshmen. That would be an enviable position for the program as it would mean any freshman who does win a starting job is a bona fide stud. Much of this hinges on Kyle Flood as a developer and a productive offseason of off-field work. Flood has a lot to prove in Year 2. Offensive line coaches must show progress with what they inherit, not just what they recruit. No one has a five year timeline to see results except psychics and Whoopi Goldberg's personal trainer.

The potential inadequacy of the Texas offensive line is really a fear of pass protection capabilities, primarily at tackle. While this is no small weakness to overcome, an otherwise loaded offense can find ways to relieve pressure through scheme, spreading the field, getting the ball out to great athletes in space, an explosive running game that forces edge rushers to find religion, and avoiding 3rd and long predictable pass rushing situations. The 2021 Oklahoma State Cowboys were not as loaded at the skill positions as Texas will be in 2022, went 12-2, and were inches away from a Big 12 title with the weakest overall offensive line and starting tackle combination on a 12 win team that the league has seen in some time. Though that team was driven heavily by their defense, the Cowboy offense was good enough to put double digit wins on the board and take down Notre Dame in a bowl game shootout. Flood will earn his paycheck this year, but the line needs to be only adequate in pass protection for this offense to light up most of the opponents it will face.

The Gabe Winslow Mortgage Team
832-557-1095
www.mortgagesbygabe.com
Remember, promo code: THINKING TEXAS. Hook 'em.

Defense

One of this preview's grievances with the defensive brain trust last year – other than the unit's overall performance – was in how they chose to deploy their assets, specifically the defensive line. Rather than take advantage of a relative strength, with the natural penetrators and depth to create chaos at the point of attack, they chose to largely use the interior defensive line to draw double teams, occupy space, play it straight, and set up the Longhorn linebackers, edges, and a run force safety to make plays. That is a perfectly sound defensive philosophy....if you have the players to execute it. In the absence of good or even consistent play from designated playmakers, it did not go particularly well. It was a big reason that Texas finished with the 52nd best defense in college football by FEI advanced metrics and surrendered just over 31 points per game and 426 yards per contest, while being gashed at an average of 6 yards per play. Texas allowed an unforgivable 5.2 yards per carry and 202.6 rushing yards per game, including major gashings at the hands of Arkansas (333 yards rushing) Oklahoma (339 yards rushing) and totally fell apart in key leverage situations, as in the 4th quarter against Oklahoma State in Austin where they surrendered 118 yards on 14 carries to Cowboy running back Jaylan Warren in the 4th quarter alone. In that same vein, Oklahoma won the Red River Shootout by handing the ball to Kennedy Brooks on a counter play with 3 seconds left on the clock. Brooks went untouched on a 33 yard touchdown scamper to seal Sooner victory. A remarkable way to lose to a rival and nothing short of defensive malpractice.

Too often, the Texas scheme sacrificed knights and bishops to feature pawns. Of course, the overabundance of pawns and absence of queens on the chess board was also part of the problem. No one is under the impression that the staff inherited the 2015 Denver Broncos. Building an effective defense without ideal parts is a challenge. But it is one the staff will need to meet for Texas to reach its full potential. To be clear, this preview is not arguing that Texas coaches misplayed a potential Top 10 defense. That is not a realistic assessment of the available talent. But might the team have been ranked 42nd instead of 52nd with a better disposition of assets and clearer thinking about featuring the best personnel? Might they have held Kansas to fewer than 57 points at home? Or prevented Oklahoma from scoring 25 fourth quarter points? These are not unreasonable questions.

The Texas pass defense was better than the run defense as its conservative coverages did a good job of disallowing big plays downfield (opponents averaged 7.1 yards per attempt) but they failed to turn over the quarterback (only 7 interceptions forced) and opponents completed a sizzling 67.6% of their passes and converted an alarming number of 3rd downs on seemingly gimme throws at the sticks. Given a slate of opposing quarterbacks who were something less than murderer's row, that made the lack of situational adaptation to down and distance particularly irritating. The overall pass defense strategy, In combination with a deficient rushing defense, allowed opponents to play ball control, wear down a marginally conditioned defense, and wait for the big plays to happen on simple running plays in the latter stages of the game.

Given five Longhorn losses by eight points or less, even a modest difference in defensive output could have meant a three win season swing. Yes, ladies and gentlemen, by simply improving defensive output marginally, the Longhorns could have played in the Cheez-It Bowl in Orlando, Florida. Mini-golfing capital of the world. But Texas fans had that joy stolen from them. Is there no justice?

One of Pete Kwiatkowski's strengths at prior stops was his ability to tweak his defensive philosophy to suit his personnel. Last year was a miss. This year, whatever the shortcomings of his personnel, Kwiatkowski should have a realistic assessment of what his personnel can or cannot do. Bringing former TCU head coach Gary Patterson on to the staff as a consultant to work on improving efficiencies should help. If it does not become an ego struggle. Patterson is no shrinking violet and will question a number of core assumptions that the Longhorn staff held or currently hold, whether with regards to scheme, personnel selection, practice, or the structure of the offseason program. Texas badly needs that positive tension and a devil's advocate. The defense should improve. The defense must improve. Coach K is too accomplished a defensive coordinator to keep forcing schematic square pegs into personnel round holes. Phrasing.

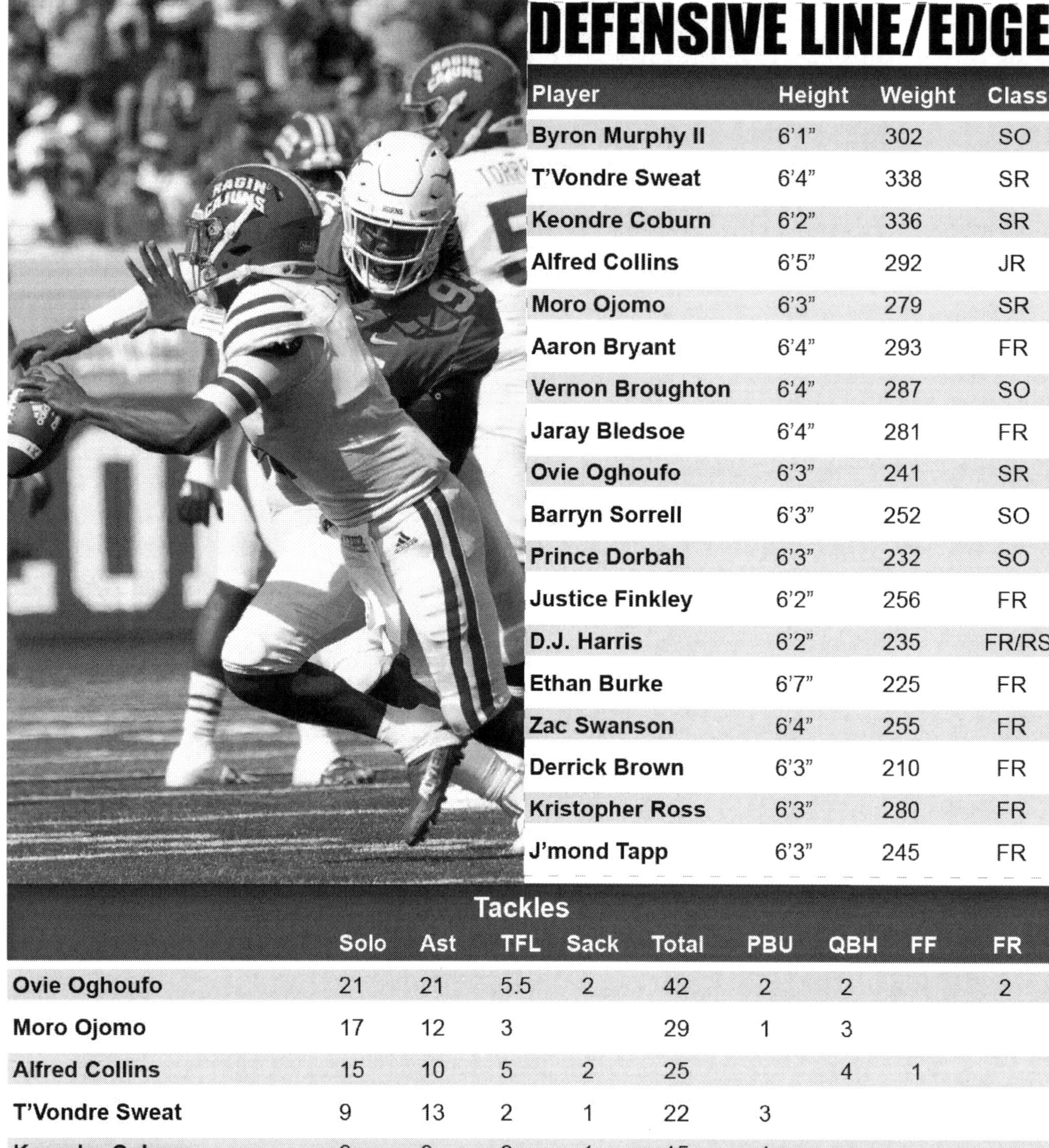

DEFENSIVE LINE/EDGE

Player	Height	Weight	Class
Byron Murphy II	6'1"	302	SO
T'Vondre Sweat	6'4"	338	SR
Keondre Coburn	6'2"	336	SR
Alfred Collins	6'5"	292	JR
Moro Ojomo	6'3"	279	SR
Aaron Bryant	6'4"	293	FR
Vernon Broughton	6'4"	287	SO
Jaray Bledsoe	6'4"	281	FR
Ovie Oghoufo	6'3"	241	SR
Barryn Sorrell	6'3"	252	SO
Prince Dorbah	6'3"	232	SO
Justice Finkley	6'2"	256	FR
D.J. Harris	6'2"	235	FR/RS
Ethan Burke	6'7"	225	FR
Zac Swanson	6'4"	255	FR
Derrick Brown	6'3"	210	FR
Kristopher Ross	6'3"	280	FR
J'mond Tapp	6'3"	245	FR

	Tackles								
	Solo	Ast	TFL	Sack	Total	PBU	QBH	FF	FR
Ovie Oghoufo	21	21	5.5	2	42	2	2		2
Moro Ojomo	17	12	3		29	1	3		
Alfred Collins	15	10	5	2	25		4	1	
T'Vondre Sweat	9	13	2	1	22	3			
Keondre Coburn	9	6	2	1	15	1			
Byron Murphy II	10	5	3.5	2	15				
Barryn Sorrell	3	4	1		7				

Can God create a Coburn that he could not lift? Whether it was Thomas Aquinas or the Thinking Texas Football preview that first posed this important theological question is immaterial. What does matter is getting more lift from the play of the 5th year senior nose tackle in 2022. Now a grizzled veteran with 33 starts under his belt (well, more likely suspenders), **Keondre Coburn** took a step back last year in his play. The culprit is not clear, but the surmise is that Coburn attempted to drop weight before the 2021 season the wrong way (dieting, not lifting) and the only thing he managed to really drop was his strength.

That is not a good idea in an anaerobic sport, much less at a position that puts a premium on maximizing force production against an external resistance. Last year, Coburn struggled to maintain low pads or exert much force at the point of attack beyond a snap or two a series. His pass rush consisted mostly of 8th grade school dance swaying with the opposing center. An athlete with Coburn's potential should be collapsing pockets when blocked 1 on 1, not making truces. He finished the season with 15 tackles, 2 for loss. Though meager statistics can be very deceptive at nose tackle, his subjective play mirrored his worst statistical year as a starter. If Coburn's deficits from last year can be addressed, it is key to keep Keondre's snap count reasonable so that his motor can rev consistently rather than overplaying him and seeing his gas tank come up empty. Defensive line coach Bo Davis knows that Coburn playing 25 or 30 maniacal snaps per game will create better total outcomes than the accumulated fatigue of an every down player who bursts between 50-100% output over 50 snaps. Given the depth on the Longhorn defensive line, Texas should focus on playing Coburn very hard on limited snaps. Word is that Coburn is in the best shape of his life right now, but if he sacrificed strength for numbers on a scale, Texas will need to feature more T'Vondre Sweat

T'Vondre Sweat was effectively a co-starter with Keondre Coburn at nose tackle last year and was generally more effective overall. Why Coburn kept earning the starting nod over Sweat is anyone's guess, but snaps matter more than starts.

Last year, Sweat compiled 22 tackles, 2 of them for loss, and he has now appeared in 35 games as a Longhorn. The former Huntsville defensive end is a massive athlete and now weighs a full Coburn. Or does Coburn weigh an entire Sweat? Whatever your preferred unit of weight, Texas fans are tired of the wait for Sweat to live up to his NFL potential. Sweat often does a fine job of resetting the line of scrimmage in the Longhorn's favor from his nose tackle position and he can play 3 technique when the Horns want to bully an undersized guard, but his NFL potential will only be realized if he plays his final season on the 40 Acres like a contract year with all of the urgency that entails. Sweat has the second brightest NFL future (behind Alfred Collins) of the core Longhorn veteran defensive linemen, but why that has not yet translated to more consistent game impact is an interesting question.

Moro Ojomo is another experienced veteran, a 5th year player who has started 25 games during his time in Austin. Despite that tenure, Ojomo is actually much younger than his peers, having begun kindergarten at age 4 in Lagos, Nigeria.

Consequently, he is at least one or two full years younger than his classmates. In 2020, he started nine games at strongside defensive end, more out of desperation than fit. The edge is not Ojomo's natural position and though he acquitted himself fairly well with 21 tackles, 2 sacks, and 3 quarterback hurries, the 2021 move back inside to 3 technique promised to unleash his compact quickness and motor on less athletic offensive linemen. Well, that was the hope. Unfortunately, Ojomo was again miscast, not by position, but by schematic disposition. Texas largely chose to eschew defensive penetration and attempted to occupy blockers to free up the linebackers and safeties to make plays. Ojomo embraced his role, but it did not play to his strengths or his 6-2, 275 pound frame. Ojomo started 12 games and tallied 29 tackles with a meager 3 tackles for loss on the year. During the 2022 offseason, the disciplined and academically inclined Ojomo (he is a finance major) called out several of his teammates for focusing on distractions over maximizing themselves as football players. On one hand, he violated the sanctity of the locker room. A football taboo. On the other hand, perhaps Ojomo had called out his teammates privately before to little effect and thought public humiliation was the spur needed for peers who value social media likes and follows more than the respect of their teammates. Perhap Ojomo's frustrations stem not just from the underachievement of some of his peers, but his own utilization over the last two seasons in an underperforming defense.

Alfred Collins is the best pure talent on the defensive line. Naturally, he was relegated to spot duty off of the bench until the Oklahoma State game. That would be the seventh game of the 2021 season. In his first start of the year, Collins played out of position on the edge in a four man front and looked like the best pure talent on the defense. Collins went on to start four games last year, amassing 25 tackles, 5 tackles for loss, two sacks, and four quarterback hurries. A former basketball standout, Collins has unusual coordination and movement for an athlete of his size, but he does need work on staying low, shedding blocks, hand placement, and understanding how blockers are attacking him. Collins can play disruptive 3 technique (outside shoulder of the guard), but he has the athletic ability to be employed throughout Pete Kwiatkoswki's multiple defensive fronts, including on the edge. That may be his best team use this year, given a paucity of viable edge options. Collins can do whatever he is asked to do, but he is at his best attacking and penetrating, creating tackles for loss, batting down balls, and impacting the pocket in the passing game. If a defensive scheme cannot find a role for Alfred Collins, perhaps the problem is not Collins, but the scheme.

Byron Murphy was a very pleasant surprise as a true freshman last year. He also served as an interesting control in a larger experiment.

Why would an 18 year old true freshman from a traditional high school basic strength program at Desoto show better strength at the point of attack, motor, conditioning, and pad level than a number of experienced Longhorn defensive linemen who had spent the entire offseason in the Texas S&C program? Those are the sorts of uncomfortable questions fans and media like to gloss over, but not answering those queries is precisely why Texas football is in its fourth rebuild since 2011. The 6-1, 300 pound Murphy garnered 15 tackles, 3.5 tackles for loss and had two sacks in limited snaps. He was the best interior pass rusher on the defensive line and consistently showed the best overall effort.

Murphy must see the field, even if it is at the expense of more experienced veterans and program sacred cows.

Vernon Broughton is a raw athlete still learning the game and how his leverages work on a football field. Broughton demonstrates explosiveness out of his stance and is capable of a good initial strike on blockers, but he needs to learn to continue to play through contact and not wilt when the encounter moves to a more prolonged engagement phase. His two primary deficits are physical strength and pad level. That could be said of several Texas players last year. The latter criticism was particularly noticeable in Broughton. Vernon is a good athlete learning to be a football player and there is still time for the sophomore to grow into his own.

Edge

Ovie Oghoufo demonstrated quickness off the edge in his 8 starts last year, amassing 42 tackles and 2 sacks, but he was poor against the run and consistently ran too far up field and lost containment on scrambling quarterbacks, draw plays, and zone read.

He also played smaller than his listed 240 pounds at the point of attack. Oghoufo returns for his 5th season of college football and will again compete for a starting role. He needs more physicality, pure strength, and better awareness and discipline if he wants to be a difference maker. If he does not start, at minimum, he is a viable situational pass rusher and depth asset.

Barryn Sorrell had a strong offseason and spring scrimmage and will press for a starting role this year. The New Orleans native showed some ability as a freshman during spot duty, but his ability to play the run and pass rush at a decent level and a strong offseason of development have propelled him up the depth chart. Sorrell has not yet evidenced any single outstanding attribute, but his appeal is a lack of the glaring deficits that plague some of his edge peers.

Early enrollee freshman **Justice Finkley** has impressed with his maturity, focus, and developed body, but his 6-2 stocky frame means he must win as a pass rusher with motor and strength rather than elite speed or change of direction. Against higher level tackles, he will be big-brothered (imagine a kid punching the air while his bigger sibling keeps a hand on his forehead) until he can add more skills to his repertoire. While there are big expectations for Finkley at a position of dire need, Justice starting as a true freshman is probably not the good news that most fans will greet it as. He has excellent long term potential though.

DJ Harris has legitimate first step quickness, but the redshirt freshman has not had enough game reps to show what he can fully do and he is still too light to hold up consistently setting the edge in the run game. He is potentially very interesting as a situational pass rusher.

Prince Dorbah came to Texas from Highland Park as a tweener with an uncertain position projection. He is currently on the outside looking in for significant playing time.

Solid defensive line depth means that new arrivals **Aaron Bryant**, **Jaray Bledsoe**, **Kris Ross** and **Zac Swanson** are likely redshirts who will see spot action, but Bledsoe's raw athleticism suggests the highest potential for an unexpected breakout.

The Longhorns badly need answers on the edge, so the freshmen will all get auditions when they arrive this summer. **J'Mond Tapp** is a natural pass rusher with a great frame who could press for early playing time while **Derrick Brown** still needs some time to grow into his body. **Ethan Burke's** lean 6-6 frame needs additional weight and strength, but he could be a very good one, with real potential for holding 270 pounds while still maintaining quickness.

Prognosis

The staff's use of their defensive line personnel last year was disappointing. As was an offseason S&C program that did not marry to the requirements of Kwiatkowski's preferred employment of his charges. Beyond any particular scheme, being strong is fairly useful in a college football game, irrespective of defensive philosophy. Personnel deployment was also lacking. The 2021 scheme failed to find a place for Alfred Collins until the middle of the season at a spot where he had only sporadically practiced and they neutered Moro Ojomo's motor and quickness game, while placing a premium of playmaking on poor to mediocre edge play and linebackers. Coaches talk a great deal about finding their best 11 and it would be difficult to argue that the Texas staff fulfilled that goal. Similarly, the Longhorns saw veteran defensive linemen plateau or actively take a step back in their physical development and game play, which only compounded the problem. Fingers could be pointed at defensive line coach Bo Davis, and there is plenty of blame to go around, but his job is to coach the players within the proscribed scheme. And he is not tasked with S&C. Seeing true freshman three star recruit Byron Murphy outperform 4th year college players with better play strength should raise an eyebrow. In short, Pete did not play his defensive cards, however limited they were at some spots, optimally. At least up front. Head S&C coach Torre Becton did not help him execute that plan particularly well either. A C level plan that was maximized would have had better results. 2021 was a C level plan minimized. To Kwiatkoswki's credit, he tried to adjust mid season, but valuable time and planning had already been lost, replaced by ad hoc solutions.

This year, the Texas staff has no excuses. They know what their assets are on the defensive line and they know the liabilities. If they go back stubbornly to the same well, expect the same results. It seems improbable that they will do that after an offseason of reflection. Texas also successfully identified this offseason that being strong is important to football players and hired a consultant to help him make the players stronger with more core lifts.

While the 2022 Class of Beef offensive line class got all of the attention, the 2022 Texas defensive line and edge class were hardly The Class of Grief. Texas signed a terrific, balanced defensive line and edge group. Their impact will be felt soon, but probably most significantly beginning in 2023 and 2024.

LINEBACKER

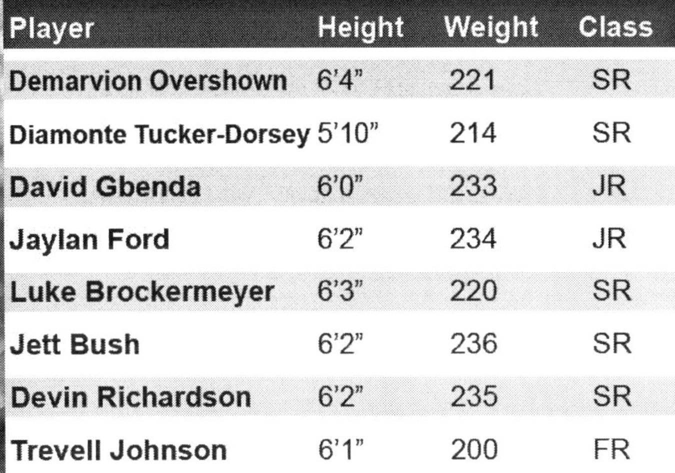

Player	Height	Weight	Class
Demarvion Overshown	6'4"	221	SR
Diamonte Tucker-Dorsey	5'10"	214	SR
David Gbenda	6'0"	233	JR
Jaylan Ford	6'2"	234	JR
Luke Brockermeyer	6'3"	220	SR
Jett Bush	6'2"	236	SR
Devin Richardson	6'2"	235	SR
Trevell Johnson	6'1"	200	FR

	Tackles								
	Solo	Ast	TFL	Sack	Total	PBU	INT	FF	FR
Diamonte Tucker-Dorsey	39	76	8.5	2.5	115		4	2	1
Demarvion Overshown	38	36	5.5	2	74	2			1
Luke Brockermeyer	36	36	5	.5	72	1	2		
Jaylan Ford	29	24	6	0	53				
David Gbenda	17	10	2.5	1.5	27	2			
Jett Bush	9	5	3.5	1	14				
Devin Richardson	3	2	0	0	5				

Demarvion Overshown led the team with 74 tackles last year, but the story of the Longhorn run defense was more often told by the tackles that he was not in position to make than the ones he did. In the offseason, a healthy Overshown filled out to 230 pounds and now looks more like a linebacker than a repurposed safety. That should help his durability and the overall physicality from the second level of defenders. It may also improve his optionality as the Texas staff comes to a different understanding of #0's best use. Overshown now has 22 cumulative career starts on his Horn resume, mostly at linebacker, most of them wearing more armbands than an Egyptian mummy, but excuses about not understanding his role are starting to wear thin.

Overshown is a very good overall athlete who excels in coverage, sprinting through a gap, or running down skill players on the edge. His best use is not much more complex than see-ball, chase-ball. Unfortunately, that is not always what the defense asked Overshown to do. Playing traditional off-ball linebacker requires reading keys and reliable decision-making. Texas needs a steady hand and finisher at linebacker and despite 2022 preseason All-Big 12 honors by preview magazines that rely more on name recognition than game film, that is not Overshown's strength. Overshown demonstrated a suboptimal understanding of reads and there were a few big opponent running plays where Overshown was the absent run force. Overshown has not been a particularly tenacious student of the game, so it is on the coaches to craft a specific role for him that keeps things basic. Or reimagine his role entirely.

Along those lines, the coaches have begun to experiment with Overshown as a hybrid edge player. On one play, he will be lined up on the edge, on another, he will be off the ball, peeking into the backfield at an angle rather than in the middle of the maelstrom. The idea is that he will be reacting to a much cleaner picture and his athleticism will carry him to the football. The truth is that while Overshown looks the part and moves like a player who should make an impact, as a linebacker he is an inconsistent high beta performer capable of game-changing highs but more often forehead slapping lows. That can be mitigated at a hybrid or edge position where the athlete has distance from the ball (with accompanying perspective) and can be offered a single discrete task (go cover that guy, blitz that gap, chase the ball). Whether Texas can craft a larger defense to accommodate that is the larger question. The problem with that is at what point is the staff letting the tail wag the dog in how they are structuring the defense overall? Is Demarvion so special that Texas must build out the defense around his attributes? What is clear is that inconsistency at the tackling end of the inside linebacker funnel makes the entire Kwiatkoswki scheme fall apart. Overshown has impact potential, but it is time the senior's play matched his press. That will come with the coaches either crafting him a more forgiving role, Overshown growing his own game as a traditional linebacker, or the staff realizing that they may be better off with unremarkable and steady athletes over a mercurial wildcard who cannot execute what they want. All of those considerations are not mutually exclusive ideas.

David Gbenda is an undersized 4th year junior linebacker with good mobility who will compete for a starting job. The squatty but quick Gbenda fits the mold of the spread-busting linebacker archetype that proliferates in the Big 12, but linebacker coach Jeff Choate must work with him on recognition and ball awareness. Gbenda had some odd instances last year where he ran away from the football, most notably against Arkansas, Oklahoma and in the second half of the Oklahoma State game. Gbenda's positive attributes are that he has been a sure tackler when he makes the right read, he is physically tough and scrappy, and he is very solid in coverage. Those mistakes are likely teachable moments and there is little doubt that Gbenda is contending for a starting job and, failing that, would be the first linebacker off of the bench.

Jaylan Ford logged considerably more playing time as the season progressed due to Luke Brockermeyer's injuries and general dissatisfaction with the play of the starting linebackers.

The third year inside linebacker has only three career starts, but by season's end, he was the most instinctive and reliable linebacker on the team. Those attributes are not paired with high level athleticism, but there are ways to make Ford's responsibilities narrow and executable that do not require him to be a NFL combine freak. Ford finished 3rd on the team in tackles with 53 and led all Texas defenders with 6 tackles for loss. That latter statistic, while tantamount to being valedictorian at summer school for a Texas defense that made shockingly few plays on the opponent's side of the line, does speak to Ford's natural timing and instinct for taking a gap, rather than elite quickness. He will certainly vie for a starting job and if he can continue to maximize his body, Ford's steady play may be exactly what the doctor ordered. Ford was the most productive linebacker on the team from the Oklahoma State game on and it is a good bet that his play and a solid offseason will earn him a starting role in the season opener.

Diamonte Tucker-Dorsey transferred to Texas from James Madison and Texas defensive coordinator Pete Kwiatkowski hopes that Diamonte can improve the constitution of the Longhorn defense and draft a bill of rights that forbids offensive overreach against the citizens of Longhorn nation. The undersized linebacker (5-10, 215) led the FCS playoff program in tackles and generally stuffed the box score every week with 116 tackles, 4 interceptions, 2.5 sacks, 4 pass break ups and 6 quarterback hurries. Not bad at all. Is he a Diamonte in the rough? Maybe. His film shows good eye discipline and ball awareness lined up as a traditional linebacker or as a hybrid run oriented safety (he played the HERO position – effectively a combo of both positions) and he demonstrates natural coverage skills in space. However, he is an average athlete in terms of speed or explosiveness by FBS standards and it is unknown how he will adapt his game to a more conventional linebacker role at 215 pounds. At minimum, Diamonte provides more depth and optionality for a Texas defense hunting for reliability and soundness at the second level of the defense. Whether he is a diamond or coal will be proved between the lines.

Devin Richardson transferred in from New Mexico State before the 2021 season and saw only spot action last year. The now Texas senior was a freshman All-American in 2019 when he racked up 69 tackles, 3 forced fumbles, and 2 sacks in his debut as a redshirt freshman. Although that honor is certainly laudable, it is often awarded based on a narrow field of competitors rather than predictive star power. Devin Richardson is a below average athlete in space and we need more game action to assess his abilities as a more conventional run stopper between the tackles. In the spring game, Roschon Johnson put an ankle breaking move on him in the flat that belonged on an And1 mixtape. Ideally, Richardson is a depth piece.

Luke Brockermeyer is a former walk-on, son of Longhorn Hall of Fame standout offensive tackle Blake Brockermeyer and a third generation Longhorn football player. Luke started ten games last year, playing most of those games with a significant upper body injury before losing the season to a torn ACL in a late November practice. Brockermeyer still finished second on the team in tackles (72) and was the best coverage linebacker on the team, at least in terms of recognition and awareness (he nabbed two interceptions on the year). Brockermeyer is a misunderstood athlete, at least in terms of his strengths.

He is a finesse, quickness-based linebacker and a good all around athlete, but he lacks strength, size, and power at the point of attack. When shielded, he can be very effective, but as injuries mounted, his physicality diminished, his tackling fell off a cliff, and he struggled in all phases. A linebacker with Luke's play style needs a certain amount of body weight armor to make it through the season and that should be an offseason focus. Unfortunately, Brockermeyer missed all of the spring rehabbing his knee and while he may be available in August, there is a wide gap between availability and readiness.

Walk-on **Jett Bush** is back to his natural position at off-the-ball linebacker after spending 2021 playing edge where he racked up 14 tackles, 3.5 tackles for loss, and a single sack. Bush lacked ideal size and length for edge play, but his motor and willingness to give up his body in the running game earned him a fair number of snaps and reminded the coaches that he might be able to help the team at his more natural position. Bush has a chance to contribute and will certainly play a role on the depth chart in his natural position.

Freshman **Trevell Johnson** is an undersized, quick linebacker who will need time in the dining hall and weight room.

Prognosis

Last year, the preview opined before the 2021 season that the major concern with the unit globally was that few of them had ever been taught to play linebacker. That may seem odd given that they had previous coaches who were being paid lots of money to teach them linebacker, but recall that former defensive coordinator and linebacker coach Todd Orlando turned the unit into robots on a joystick, executing predetermined calls that denied them developing reading and critical thinking skills, eventually just randomly run-blitzing them through a gap when he ran out of ideas. His successor Chris Ash and linebacker coach Coleman Hutszler tried to teach the game, but realized they were facing a long learning curve with COVID abbreviated practice timelines and they punted. Blaming the current group of players for their lack of football literacy is like blaming kindergartners who have never been taught phonics for their failure to read. Yelling at them to "just be football players" is as helpful as yelling at the 5 year olds to "just be readers." In the workup to 2021, the Texas linebackers struggled to do basic linebacker things. Some privately wondered if they had ever been coached a day since high school. The more instinctive linebackers who did seem to get it – namely Brockermeyer and Ford – lacked experience, size, raw talent and durability.

Linebacker coach Jeff Choate and defensive coordinator Pete Kwiatkowski have the unenviable task of flattening a learning curve. Texas coaches will have to bite the bullet and start teaching the game technically rather than just kicking the can down the road. Consequently, they will likely favor the savvier linebackers who learn more quickly, even if they have athletic deficits. But they must also craft a role for Demarvion Overshown who, despite 22 career starts, has not really demonstrated an affinity for the kind of traditional linebacking role that the defense requires. If that means starting the savviest linebackers over the ones who look better running around, so be it. But they may also want to find a simplified role for the guys who look good running around. The necessary change at linebacker must happen in three places: in the film room and on-the-field teaching, in how they conceive, craft and cast the defense, and on the recruiting trail. The first two changes are already happening, but Texas failed to address linebacker needs in the 2022 class and the portal provided only a FCS transfer.

DEFENSIVE BACK

Player	Height	Weight	Class
D'Shawn Jamison	5'10"	190	SR
Anthony Cook	6'1"	192	SR
Kitan Crawford	5'11"	198	JR
Jahdae Barron	5'11"	185	JR
Ryan Watts	6'3"	210	JR
Terrance Brooks	5'11"	210	FR
Jerrin Thompson	6'0"	185	JR
JD Coffey III	6'0"	192	SO
Jamier Johnson	6'0"	170	SO
Terrance Brooks	5'11"	210	FR
Ishmael Ibraheem	6'1"	160	FR/RS
Larry Turner-Gooden	6'0"	198	FR
B.J. Allen Jr.	6'0"	206	FR
Jaylon Guilbeau	6'0"	179	FR
Austin Jordan	6'0"	190	FR
Xavion Brice	6'1"	175	FR

	Tackles				Passes Defensed		
	Solo	Ast	TFL	Total	PBU	INT	TD
D'Shawn Jamison	34	14	0	48	1	1	0
Anthony Cook	27	20	3	47	3	0	0
Jerrin Thompson	26	15	3	41	3	1	0
Jahdae Barron	12	6	1	18	3	0	0
JD Coffey III	2	3	0	5	0	0	0
Kitan Crawford	5	0	0	5	0	0	0

D'shawn Jamison is back and the 5th year veteran cornerback now boasts 48 game appearances and 31 starts in his Longhorn career. The promise of D'shawn Jamison's true impact as a ball hawk has been seemingly deferred for three years running. Is 2022 the year it happens? Last year, he totaled 48 tackles and one interception. While Jamison's consistency as a tackler improved, a fairly conservative off-coverage scheme limited his ability to jump routes. Jamison has great quickness and good ball skills but unless the Texas defensive philosophy gets more disguise and evolves beyond teaching corners to keep the ball in front of them, Jamison may not have the best platform for showcasing his skills.

That written, it is interesting that Jamison has only 4 career interceptions in his 31 starts playing in a variety of schemes and systems. Are you a playmaker if you do not make many plays? Though Jamison has average size and physicality for the position, he possesses elite agility, in addition to the episodic amnesia that the position demands. This is Jamison's money year and Texas needs a big senior season from their most experienced starting defensive back.

Ryan Watts transferred to Texas from Ohio State (he nabbed 2 interceptions in spot action) where he was more or less their #3 cornerback and the big junior appears to have the inside track starting opposite Jamison. The big cornerback from West Elm, TX is around 6-2, 210 and has drawn praise for his physicality and length. Watts does not possess great speed, but if he can do his work early rerouting receivers and changing the timing of the offense, he will be just fine. His impact should also be felt as a tackler in run support against teams seeking to exploit the edge as well as being a capable situational blitzer off of the edge. In the spring game, he looked solid and had no problem carrying receivers upfield on deep routes. There is some thought of playing Watts at safety to take advantage of his tackling, size and lateral range, but that move will only be considered if another cornerback can play at a high level in his stead. Do not discount the possibility of that shift, but for now Watts is likely a starting cornerback.

Jahdae Barron is one of the quickest defensive backs on the team and is currently slated for a starting role at nickel. Barron can also play cornerback and it is possible that the coaches could start him there if they see excellent nickel play from another candidate and like what Ryan Watts offers at safety. The junior from Pflugerville Connally drew a lot of offseason praise for his awareness and ability to close quickly on the ball. If Barron can own the nickel position and has the pure coverage tenacity to lock up an inside receiver without needing safety help over the top, the Texas coverage defense will be able to show a lot more looks and demonstrate far less predictability in general. Some insiders believe that Barron is potentially a breakout star, but with only two career starts on his resume that is more optimistic trait protection than a track record guaranteeing certitude.

Anthony Cook is a 5th year defensive back who was a bright spot at nickel last year. While Cook did have a safety cover on most downs, he was an aggressive force, did a nice job within his taskings, tackled well, and did not bust assignments.

With the emergence of Jahdae Barron at nickel, the coaches examined the safety depth chart, considered Cook's maturity and experience, and asked him to make the move to safety. Cook did just that and has shown signs of adapting to it quickly. The veteran has 46 career game appearances and 15 starts and he should provide more field awareness and better tackling than his predecessors in 2021. Cook will certainly battle for a starting role and likely has the inside track as of this preview's writing. It very nearly was not so. Cook entered the portal in the summer of 2020, but eventually returned and now enters his final season at the University of Texas.

Kitan Crawford has the athleticism and physicality that coaches love. He is also one of the finest pure athletes on the team.

The third year defensive back has spent most of his Longhorn career at cornerback, but he was moved to safety in an attempt to create more playmaking and dynamism there. Crawford has an extensive offensive background from high school and demonstrates better than average ball skills and hands. Crawford has more than enough physicality, runs very well, and likes to hit, so what is not to love? Mainly, his comfort level at his new spot. He had some struggles in the spring identifying his responsibilities and there is an understandable learning curve for him at safety that is creating hesitation in his play. Crawford's learning curve will determine whether he is a 2022 starter and there is still a possibility that he returns to cornerback if the team suffers injuries there. Crawford has a lot of desirable traits that the coaches want out on the field, but the coaches cannot trade busted coverages and open receivers to get them.

Jerrin Thompson has started eight games in his Longhorn career. Last year, he registered 41 tackles over 12 games with 6 total starts. Thompson is not a big safety, but he embraces contact.

Unfortunately, physics does not care much about embracing and the hard math of velocity and mass reveals that a safety who weighs 178 pounds and lacks power is not going to have an easy time bringing down a 210 pound running back running with a head of steam. Thompson gained some weight this offseason and that should improve his tackling and overall durability. The want-to is there, it just needs a more robust delivery system. While Thompson does not possess any one particularly outstanding physical attribute, he is heady, possesses solid lateral range, and as he progresses physically, he has the opportunity to become a quality starting safety. Thompson is in a battle for a starting job that will continue well into August camp.

Morice Blackwell transitioned from linebacker to safety so the Horns could get better physicality and tackling there. The Longhorn spring game revealed why the staff made that move. Blackwell had a pair of slobber knocking hits and generally showed a degree of physicality at safety that was wanting last year. That will get him on the field. How long will he stay on the field? That depends on his coverage ability. In the spring game, Blackwell did not show natural coverage skills. That is likely a work in progress, but there is no doubt that Blackwell brings the wood well.

JD Coffey shares a similar frame and attributes to Jerrin Thompson, but with less game experience. Coffey will be for closers if he can add strength, progress in his understanding of the scheme, and get more live fire reps.

Jamier Johnson is a skinny sophomore who has responded favorably to coaching. An undersized recruit, Johnson committed to Texas without ever visiting the campus, making his evaluation off of a series of Zoom sessions. In the absence of game action, there are not many judgments to be made on Johnson yet, but Texas badly needs nickel and cornerback depth to develop behind Jamison, Watts and Barron.

Cornerback **Ishmael Ibraheem** is currently suspended and his status is under review.

Jaylon Guillbeau and **Terrance Brooks** are both early enrollee freshmen cornerbacks who reported in January and will have an opportunity to break into the depth chart. There may not be much choice, given the thin number of bodies available. Freshman safety **B.J. Allen** looks the part and has a promising future at safety. **Larry Turner-Gooden** reported a bit out of shape, but has already leaned up. Speedy freshman **Austin Jordan** can play either cornerback or safety.

Prognosis

Drafting new blood from other positions, another year in the scheme, and progress from the returning safeties means that Texas should get better safety play than what they saw in 2022. Though that is not a hard bar to clear. Better may not necessarily mean good, but the Texas coaches will settle for competent. Cornerback and nickel are fairly straightforward. If Texas stays healthy there, there is an opportunity for elevated play, particularly if the defense can find a pass rush and the Longhorn defense is better able to embrace more disguise and scheme variation. While the 2021 pass defense did not surrender an inordinate number of big passing plays, a pervasive low risk, off-coverage philosophy allowed a high level of opponent efficiency in the passing game in addition to a maddening number of 3rd and medium plays which saw cornerbacks in off coverage with two safeties deep, effectively conceding a wide open throw to the sticks and a new set of downs. Depth at cornerback is largely unproven. True freshmen and untested sophomores must step up. While the Longhorn staff does not have an elite corps of defensive backs, there should be enough material here to put together an effective pass defense.

SPECIAL TEAMS

Player	Height	Weight	Class
Will Stone	6'0"	175	FR
Bert Auburn	6'0"	180	FR/RS
Isaac Pearson	6'2"	213	FR/RS

Texas finished ranked 11th in the country in special teams by advanced metrics, almost entirely on the strength of an exceptional senior year from departed double duty kicker and punter Cameron Dicker, with a special assist from the Longhorn punt blocking team. Dicker converted on 87% of his field goals, averaged over 46 yards per punt, and showed a big leg on kickoffs. Dicker's hang time and directional ability on punts also contributed to Texas punt coverage limiting opponents to a paltry 2.8 yards per return with a season long return of 9 yards. However, outside of Dicker, and three blocked opponent punts, special teams performance ranged from middling to troubling. Texas punt returns, kick returns, and kick coverage were not particularly good. Primary punt returner D'shawn Jamison averaged only 8.8 yards per return and if you remove his 43 yard return against Texas Tech, his average return drops to around 5.6 yards per punt return. Kickoff returns were also quite poor. Texas struggled to block for Xavier Worthy and D'shawn Jamison and showed poor coordination overall. Longhorn returners averaged a meager 19.38 yards per return, meaning any kick returned from the goal line cost Texas an average of six yards of field position. Unfortunately, Texas opponents averaged a robust 26.2 yards per kickoff return, including an 87 yard return by the TCU Horned Frogs. Texas has a lot of work to do on their return and coverage teams, but how will Texas replace Dicker?

Texas will start its third Australian punter in the last five years in the form of ProKick Australia graduate Isaac Pearson. Pearson is another former Australian Rules Football player who realized that he could get a free education and use his accent to meet American women by kicking a ball three or four times a game without even getting hit. Fair dinkum! Pearson is said to have a kangaroo leg, but expect the typical Year 1 Aussie growing pains that come with their first live action, complete with fumbled snaps and occasional shanks. It happened to Dickson, it happened to Bujcevski, it will happen to Pearson. The good news is that Pearson was the top rated prospect for ProKick Australia in the 2021 class and it should click for him soon enough.

Sideshow Bert Auburn has the inside track on kicking duties, but true freshman Will Stone should challenge. Auburn saw very limited action last year and he is a bit of an unknown. His main pros are a promising high school career at Flower Mound Marcus and perhaps the finest Caucasian afro in all of college sports. Given the potential explosiveness of the Texas offense and Auburn's inexperience and more limited range vis a vis Dicker, the mathematics underpinning 4th and 4 on the opponent 32 yard line becoming a go-for-it situation rather than a likely field goal attempt may work out just fine.

Louisiana Monroe Warhawks

September 3 | Austin, TX

Sun Belt Conference
Terry Bowden | 2nd season

2021 Record	3-yr Trend	5-yr Trend
4-8	9-25	19-39

Returning Starters	Offense	Defense
10	6	4

Overview

The Warhawks have been a moribund program since they started playing football in 1975. The zenith of program success was a 8-5 record in 2012 under head coach Todd Berry, a season which included a heady win over Arkansas in their season opener, close shootout losses to Auburn and Baylor, and then a blowout defeat against the Ohio Bobcats in the Independence Bowl. That season was the program's Bright Shining Moment. Louisiana-Monroe boasts an all-time program winning percentage around 35% and serves as the doormat of the Sun Belt conference in more years than not. Seasoned head coach Terry Bowden (175-114-2 lifetime record) took over last year to change their fortunes and did not have much success, despite having spread option wizard Rich Rodriguez as his offensive coordinator. Rodriguez has since traveled further down the boulevard of broken dreams to the head coaching job at Jackson State, leaving Bowden to figure out how he wants to wind out the string on his last collegiate job after going 4-8 overall and 2-6 in league play in his first season.

Terry, son of legendary Florida State head coach Bobby Bowden, is an interesting character and coaching survivor who first rose to national prominence at Auburn where he led the Tigers to their longest win streak in school history along with an impressive streak of NCAA violations. He inherited a program on probation and left them that way. Paying it forward, the Auburn way. He left in scandal, as any self-respecting Auburn football coach does, which included accusations of an affair with the daughter of Auburn's most prominent and kingmaking booster, Bobby Lowder. There's dipping your pen in the company ink and then there's painting a billboard with it and hanging it on the highway. The colorful head coach once related that when he got the Auburn job, he was handed a list of players who were being paid and what each was making. He studied it intently and frowned. “What's the matter coach, are you upset that we're paying guys?" Bowden responded,"No, you're paying the wrong ones." Right now, Bowden would not mind paying to get some better talent to Monroe, Louisiana (how can they not find a defense contractor to sponsor the Warhawks? Your move, Northropp Grumann) as the current roster lacks quality, depth, and impact players. It is never a good idea to overlook an opponent, particularly for a Texas program that has managed to lose to Kansas twice in the last five years, but Louisiana-Monroe is going to be a pretty terrible football team. They do feature a large number of Texas native born athletes, so they will certainly be up for the contest on September 3rd in Austin. Nonetheless, if Texas struggles too much with the Warhawks in their season opener, turn this preview into a fireplace log and take up another hobby.

Strengths

Dual threat quarterback Chandler Rogers played pretty good ball for Louisiana-Monroe last year after transferring there from Blinn Junior College, despite little help from his supporting cast. Rogers completed 62.6% of his passes with a healthy 9 touchdown to 3 interception ratio and accumulated 1,311 yards passing at 7.3 yards per attempt. He also rushed 139 times for a meager 367 yards, though sacks were responsible for winnowing down his 2.6 yards per carry average. The 6-0, 190 pound native of Mansfield, TX is a game competitor, but he is being asked to carry a burden that few quarterbacks could shoulder. He will have a fine receiving target in the fantastically named slot receiver Boogie Knight. Boogie caught 45 balls for 588 yards and 3 touchdowns last year, earning All-Sunbelt honors. There are probably a number of surprising things about a guy named Boogie Knight, beginning with speculation about just how much his parents loved Paul Thomas Anderson and ending with the fact that he is a white kid from Akron, Ohio. Disappointingly, the Warhawk media guide reveals that his given name is Jeremiah and his major is criminal justice, not film.

The Warhawks were the least penalized teams in college football, averaging less than four per game and ranking ahead of the service academies. Penalties as a shorthand for discipline and focus is a long established football platitude but its correlation to winning in 2021 was complex. The second least penalized team in college football? The Kansas Jayhawks.

Weaknesses

The offensive line returns only two starters from a unit that was ranked 129th out of 130 FBS schools in rushing success. For an offense built around the spread running game, that is suboptimal. They also gave up 39 sacks and 104 tackles for loss. Unsurprisingly, the Warhawks were dead last in the Sun Belt in total scoring and yards gained. By advanced metrics, they ranked 111th out of 130 FBS schools in overall offensive efficiency.

Defensively, the Warhawks finished ranked 105th by advanced metrics, allowing 33.5 points per game and 290 passing yards per contest. Opposing quarterbacks enjoyed great efficiency last year, completing over 67% of their passes while throwing for a combined 30 touchdowns at 8.35 yards per attempt. The rushing defense flirted with mediocrity, allowing 4.4 yards per attempt, but the inability to rush the passer or cover doomed the Warhawks into surrendering 6.3 yards per snap.

Breaking down the Warhawks player by player is not a particularly useful exercise. This game will be determined more by Longhorn energy, focus, and effort than anything Louisiana-Monroe does.

Alabama Crimson Tide

September 10 | Austin, TX

Southeastern Conference
Nick Sabam | 16th season

2021 Record	3-yr Trend	5-yr Trend
13-2	37-4	64-6
Returning Starters	**Offense**	**Defense**
13	5	8

Overview

Nick Saban has built a juggernaut in Tuscaloosa, leading the most dominant college football epoch in the annals of the game. As evidenced by his remarkable 178-25 record and six national titles at Alabama. Add another title at LSU and you have a compelling argument that Saban is the most accomplished college football coach of all time. At age 70, he is showing no signs of slowing down. A masterful program builder, Saban has evolved with the times as a coach, recruiter, and staff manager, showing remarkable adaptability to cutting edge trends and staff composition and turnover, while still maintaining core beliefs centered around toughness, unselfishness, and the Bama Machine being bigger than any one player or coach. Saban has little sentimentality for how he thinks the game should be played and adapts both on and off the field to its requirements like a young, hungry innovator rather than a self-satisfied legend. Last year, Alabama fell short in the national title game against Georgia, a rematch of the SEC title game that they won just a month earlier. Whether that was because of a flip of the coin in the matchup going heads instead of tails, Alabama's key injuries, or Georgia finally realizing that they had more NFL talent on the field than the Tide does not matter much to Saban. He will shrug, continue his process, and expect to be there again.

Saban has good reason to believe that. This Alabama team is deeply experienced, has a Heisman trophy winning QB, a dominant defense, and layers of well-conditioned and developed program talent that few teams can even approach. The Tide will return 8 defensive starters, two All-American pass rushers, their best inside linebacker and their entire secondary to a unit that was ranked 6th in the nation by advanced metrics. Eight of those 11 starters are seniors, including 80% of the secondary. Don't expect Alabama's defense to beat itself anytime soon. Offensively, they have a battle tested

Heisman quarterback that helped propel them to the 2nd ranked offense (40 points and 488 yards per game) in the country by advanced statistics. While Alabama will see a complete turnover of the wide receiver corps, since 2019, the Tide have had six receivers drafted. Five of them in the first round. One in the second. Are we to believe that the talent spigot has simply been shut off in Tuscaloosa? Expect a few early growing pains from the Bama pass catchers, but their stars will rise with opportunity, just like their predecessors. Alabama has enough elite players without the help of the portal, but unsurprisingly Nick Saban is becoming a master of that talent procurement tool as well. During the offseason, the Tide snagged elite runner Jahmyr Gibbs from Georgia Tech, stole former LSU starting cornerback Eli Ricks, secured Louisville deep threat Tyler Harrell (18 catches for 6 touchdowns at 29.1 yards per grab), and in the ultimate sign of the mercenary times, lured Georgia wide receiver and speedster Jermaine Burton (53 catches, 901 yards, 8 touchdowns total over his last two years) to Tuscaloosa moments after the national title game was over. Benedict Arnold thinks Burton lacks loyalty, but the Tide are not going to have a speed deficit anywhere in their offense. For good measure, they added starting offensive lineman Tyler Steen from Vanderbilt. Leave it to Nick Saban to field a Top 2 team and then hit the transfer portal relentlessly until it becomes the 2022 consensus preseason national champion in the opinion of this preview.

On September 10, in front of 105,000+, Texas will have an opportunity to make a statement against the best team on the Longhorn schedule and the best team in the country. Is this the seminal moment where the Longhorns turn their own program tide? Or will the game be a reminder of just how far the Texas program still has to go against the nationally elite?

Strengths

The Tide feature the best pair of edge rushers in college football and second place is not real close. Consensus 1st Team All-American Will Anderson had 102 tackles, 17.5 sacks, and an amazing 34.5 tackles for loss last year for the Tide. The 6-4, 240 pound outside linebacker will be a Top 3 NFL draft pick. Anderson brings elite quickness, skill, motor, and speed to the edge and the Bama run defense. Anderson is a top notch pass rusher and may even be more disruptive running down offensive players in backside pursuit or shooting gaps as a zone run disruptor. Like the Diophantine equation, Anderson is a problem to which there is no evident solution, particularly given that he is bookended by a potentially better athlete. An injury thrust sophomore Dallas Turner into a starting role last year as a freshman and the former 5 star recruit from Florida took to the position over the course of the year, notching 8.5 sacks, 10 tackles for loss and 5 hits on the quarterback. Most notably, all of his sacks came in the final seven games of the season. Turner is just starting to figure it out and with an entire offseason under his belt, he may no longer consent to being the junior member in the Anderson-Turner partnership. Turner has similar physical measurables to Anderson, but is actually a step faster. 245 pound outside linebackers that run a 4.5 40 do not grow on trees. But apparently they do in Tuscaloosa. If Turner and Anderson are not enough of a problem, the Tide love backup outside linebacker Chris Braswell (a former five star recruit) enough that they plan to run him out there on passing downs next to Anderson and Turner, giving the Tide the best pass rush in college football.

The Tide defense should be the best unit in the country. Inside linebacker Henry To'oTo'o brings hits to (t'o'o) opposing runners harder than his apostrophe game and the leading tackler for the Tide is a four year starter (two years at Tennessee, two at Bama) who has seen and done it all. The Alabama defensive line features three starting seniors in nose tackle DJ Dale and defensive ends Byron Young and Justin Eboigbe. They all fit the profile of the current incarnation of Bama defensive lineman: 290-305 pounds, great play strength and pad level, and a ton of experience. They sacrifice playmaking to free up the stars of the defense, but are capable of making impact plays if an offensive line lacks the requisite physicality to hang with them. Depth is excellent behind them as well. The Tide secondary is led by 210 pound senior strong safety Jordan Battle and he contributed 3 interceptions last year along with 84 tackles. The Tide are expecting sweet things from cornerback Kool-Aid McKinstry, a former five star recruit who is believed to be Saban's next great lockdown corner. The 6-1, 190 pound Kool-Aid is built even longer than his stature and demonstrates effortless recovery out of his breaks. LSU transfer Eli Ricks will vie for the other cornerback spot with Khyree Jackson. Nickel Brian Branch is beloved by the Tide coaches for his heady play and versatility.

You know a defense is pretty good when the Heisman winning quarterback gets second billing in the write-up of team strengths. That brings us to Bryce Young. Young cuts an unimposing physical presence (he is 6-0 in very thick socks and around 195 pounds) and he is not a dual threat runner. In fact, sometimes his lack of physical presence looks out of place on the field. Until he throws the ball. Then it all makes sense. Young can flat out throw the rock. With surprising velocity and strength, despite his diminutive stature. Young is fearless about fitting the pigskin into tight windows at improbable angles and though that can occasionally get him into trouble, his belief in his arm is well-founded. A natural leader, Young also has touch, anticipation, and a great feel for coverages. Last year, he completed 67% of his passes for 4,872 yards, 47 touchdowns, and only 7 interceptions at 8.9 yards per passing attempt. His efforts included a spectacular 559 yard passing day against the Arkansas Razorbacks, game film that the Texas coaches may not want to show to Hudson Card as a confidence builder. Young is not a run threat, both by choice and offensive design, but he is mobile enough to buy time and is fluid on the roll or on sprint-outs. He lacks the stature to have commanding vision of the field, but he has a great feel for passing windows and the Tide purposefully structure their pass blocking schemes to give him inside lanes to peer through. The best way to get Young off of his game is to seal those windows off, get push in his face, and force him to hold on to the football. There may be some validity to the idea that Young was buoyed by a pair of outstanding starting receivers in Williams and Metchie, the reliability of Slade Bolden, and an extremely supportive team infrastructure and that he could come down to earth a bit with a more inexperienced wide receiver corps. The Tide also had to throw the ball more than Nick Saban preferred, in part due to a relatively disappointing running game. The Heisman winner's pure arm talent is obvious, but NFL scouts will be taking particular note of his early season play with a less experienced supporting cast.

The rich got even richer when the Crimson Tide added transfer running back Jahmyr Gibbs, a former star at Georgia Tech. The talented multi-purpose runner from Atlanta rushed for 746 yards last year while adding another 465 yards as a pass catcher, despite playing for a miserable Yellowjacket program that finished 3-9, losing to Georgia and Notre Dame by a combined 100-0. The 5-11, 200 pounder is a slick stop-start runner, has terrific receiving skills, and is one of the premier kick returners in college football. Plagued by injuries and dissatisfied with some of the play of the runners already on campus, Saban set out to shore up a weakness and, in so doing, added another novel dimension to the offense. Expect Gibbs to play a prominent role in the Tide offense and provide serious big play capabilities.

Weaknesses

Weakness in the context of the Alabama depth chart demands a relativistic caveat, but the team is not bulletproof. Last year, the Tide running game averaged only 4.1 yards per carry and struggled repeatedly to convert on short yardage money downs on 3rd and 4th downs. Alabama still ended up converting a terrific 52% of its third downs overall, but many of those were courtesy of Bryce Young's arm. Not being able to run the ball when he wishes to do so is personally offensive to Nick Saban and this was a personal source of irritation throughout the Bama season. The blame falls primarily on three culprits: a dropoff of execution on the offensive line, a diminishment in running back talent, and Bill O'Brien's less than total dedication to using his running schemes as something more than a placeholder for the next throw.. The first issue will be addressed by new bodies, practice emphasis, and offseason S&C. The second issue will be addressed by the incoming transfer of Jahmyr Gibbs and the development of Jase McClelan and Trey Sanders. The third? A stern talking-to. The Alabama offensive line was also not seamless in pass protection. The Tide gave up 41 sacks in 15 games and four or more sacks in five of their contests. Some of that can be pinned on Bryce Young's desire to hold on to the football when he sees a potential big play opportunity, but new offensive line coach Eric Wolford (formerly offensive line coach at Kentucky) will have an opportunity to address these issues or may be encouraged to seek alternative employment like the prior one year wonder position coach Doug Marrone.

The Tide defense had a relentless pass rush last year paired with a rock-ribbed run defense. The more conventional the offense and gameplan, the more that Alabama ripped apart their opponent. The Tide accumulated 57 sacks and allowed only 2.7 yards per carry, holding opponents to an average of only 86 rushing yards per contest. Only one Tide opponent, Florida, rushed for more than 150 yards against them last year and they did it running hurry-up, no-huddle from single back three wide personnel, spreading out the Tide, mystifying their run keys with option, jet and fly sweeps, and constant deception. That performance almost allowed the Gators to pull off the upset of the confounded Tide defense. That is not likely a duplicable game plan for Longhorn personnel or Steve Sarkisian. However, the Tide showed that if you can block `em up front, there are plays available in the passing game. The Tide passing defense allowed just under 7 yards per attempt to opponents along with 25 passing touchdowns. They did not always handle play action well and Alabama's physical safeties and linebackers tended to bite and allowed mediocre passing teams like Arkansas and Texas A&M to make big plays. The Tide pass defense will not be a weakness, but they are fallible and a clever schemer with good receiving options can move the ball on them if they can keep the quarterback upright. “If” is doing a lot of work in that sentence.

Conference USA
Jeff Traylor | 3rd season

UTSA Roadrunners

September 17 | Austin, TX

2021 Record	3-yr Trend	5-yr Trend
12-2	23-15	32-29

Returning Starters	Offense	Defense
13	8	5

Overview

UTSA began playing football in 2012. Before head coach Jeff Traylor arrived on campus, they boasted a 47-55 record and no conference titles. In two short years, Traylor has led the Roadrunners to a Conference USA championship and a 19-7 record. The affable and down-to-earth head coach is an East Texas legend at Gilmer, where he led the Buckeye program to three state titles and five title game appearances in 15 years. Unsurprisingly, the current stadium bears his namesake. After rejecting the advances of bigger names that wanted to hire him away, UTSA may need to petition the city of San Antonio to rebrand the Alamodome the Traylordome. Traylor is familiar to Texas fans after his two year stint in Austin where he cemented his reputation as a player's coach and master recruiter who could talk a buzzard off of a meatwagon and a vegan into having a personality. After stops at Arkansas and SMU, Traylor got his shot in San Antonio and quickly injected the program with an energy and optimism that permeated the university. In his second year, Traylor elevated the Roadrunners to a 12-2 record and a Conference USA title that included big boy wins at Illinois and Memphis.

Traylor did an excellent job with what he inherited at UTSA and he is doing a fine job of building out the future via the portal and by leveraging his tremendous high school coaching relationships throughout the state. Timing is everything in coaching and whether Traylor looks back with regret or pride at signing a 10 year extension for 28 million dollars with a 7.5 million dollar buyout clause remains to be seen. It is clear that Traylor wants to build his own legacy in San Antonio and that is a laudable thing in a world where coaches always have one foot out of the door. It is clear that it will take a top job offer to get him out. One of those jobs is up the road in Austin and you can bet that Traylor will have a special level of motivation when he brings his Roadrunners up I-35 to face the team that introduced him to college coaching. While it would make a lot of sense for Traylor to focus on the Texas game throughout the summer to the exclusion of some early season opponents to optimize his chances for a statement game upset, a home opener against a potentially good Houston Cougars squad followed by a road trip to upstate New York against a contrarian Army option attack before traveling to Austin guarantees that Traylor will have to play it straight.

Strengths

The UTSA passing offense is loaded. They return all three starting wide receivers that put up big numbers last year in Zakhari Franklin (81 catches, 1027 yards, 12 tds), Josh Cephus (71 catches, 819 yards, 6 tds) and big possession receiver D'Corion Clark (72 catches, 755 yards, 7 tds). The three accounted for 72.7% of UTSA's receiving yards last year and should match or exceed that total in 2022. 6th year quarterback Frank Harris will orchestrate the passing game. Last year, he threw for 3177 yards and added another 566 yards rushing, accounting for 33 total touchdowns and only 6 interceptions. Harris can be a very dangerous runner, but as his passing skills have grown, the 6-0, 200 pound athlete has increasingly learned to do his primary damage through the passing game. Traylor calls him the most improved player he has ever coached. Throw in an offensive line that returns four starters and the Roadrunner offense is guaranteed to be humming early. Texas will not see an opponent passing game with more continuity, experience, and production on its schedule. Expect them to improve on a 2021 attack that averaged 36.9 points per game and finished ranked in the top 25 nationally by advanced metrics. Beyond their production against a lesser schedule, how will their raw talent stack up against the likes of Texas? We will get to find out on a Saturday in September.

The Roadrunners played tough run defense last year, allowing only 3.3 yards per carry and 114.7 yards rushing per game. This is a function of their schematic focus, featuring a 4i three man front that does a good job of clogging up running lanes, and their willingness to drop an extra safety in the box to hunt for negative plays. While UTSA's talent is not elite, the Texas offense should not confuse their run defense with a typical non Power 5 unit. They feature a number of portal transfers from major programs and their home grown run stoppers do a fine job as well.

Weaknesses

UTSA's passing defense gave up way too many big plays. In fact, the Roadrunners looked more like Wile E Coyote than their namesake against the deep ball, having allowed the most 30+ yard completions in college football over the last two seasons. The secondary needs to order new Acme Rocket Skates or start working on concepts like staying deeper than the deepest receiver. In 2021, the Roadrunners allowed a hefty 8.3 yards per attempt to opposing quarterbacks, 14.1 yards per catch to opposing receivers, and 27 passing touchdowns. Western Kentucky's Bailey Zappe exploited UTSA for 523 yards the first time they played and then lit them up for 577 a few weeks later in the Conference USA title game running the same vertical concepts in varying forms. It wasn't just Western Kentucky. 8 of 14 UTSA opponents averaged more than 8 yards per attempt. If an opponent's passing game had a pulse, the Roadrunners bled big plays downfield. That was the primary reason why their defense finished the season ranked 74th in the country by advanced metrics. They return only five starters from that unit and while new blood may be a positive, it is also pretty clear that the Roadrunner susceptibility to big passing plays is also a schematic and play calling issue. Bottom line: Steve Sarkisian and Texas need to test the Roadrunners downfield.

The preview is not being disingenuous in suggesting that Jeff Traylor may miss star running back Sincere McCormick. The gutty, talented runner amassed 1479 yards rushing last year at 5 yards a clip while adding 15 touchdowns. The 5-9, 205 pound McCormick is not a speedster (he ran a 4.6 40 at the NFL combine) but he was a steady chain mover who brought an element of ball control, balance, and tough running to an explosive offense. He was their late game closer and exhibited a knack for coming up big against the Roadrunners' toughest opponents, rushing for 117 rugged yards on 31 carries at Illinois, notching 41 carries for 184 yards on the road at Memphis, and finally, carrying UTSA to win in the conference title game with a spectacular 239 yard, 3 touchdown effort against WKU. The bigger the opponent and the tougher the environment, the more the Roadrunners leaned on their little big man. The staff is confident that talented Arkansas transfer Trelon Smith can fill the void left by McCormick, but sincerity counts for a lot more than talent on a running back's 41st carry on the road with the game on the line.

The appeal of Jeff Traylor as a program turnaround guy was his recruiting acumen, optimism, people skills, and motivational vibe. The sell to UTSA was to take your lumps for a couple of years, let the man recruit and build, and reap the benefits beginning in Year 3. Yet, UTSA was hoisting a league championship trophy in Jeff's second year on the job. Clearly, Traylor and his core staff coached the heck out of their inherited talent. In the offseason, a good chunk of that core staff departed. Offensive coordinator Barry Lunney, who was instrumental in the growth of quarterback Frank Harris, went to Illinois. Co-defensive coordinator Rod Wright (former Texas defensive tackle) left for Miami. Special teams coach Tommy Perry went to Colorado State. That sort of turnover often comes with a larger program cost. Interestingly, Traylor hired from within to replace all of his lost staff, a fairly irregular practice in college football today. Either Traylor is a loyalist to a fault who wants to prioritize cultural continuity over resume hunting, or perhaps Coach Traylor understands that he and his culture are the real straw that stirs the drink in San Antonio.

Overview

From 1993 to 2010, the Texas Tech football program never suffered a losing season. Like the Lubbock restaurant scene, the program was at no risk of earning a Michelin star, but Red Raider fans could always count on a decent meal every fall. Since firing Mike Leach in 2009, they have had a sour taste in their mouths. Tech football has gone 71-77 and managed exactly zero winning seasons in Big 12 conference play. The Panda Express of college football. And the MSG stands for Makeshift Slapdash Games. Last year Thinking Texas Football predicted that Matt Wells would not finish the year in Lubbock and he didn't even make it out of October, fired unceremoniously after a 25-24 loss to Kansas State on October 25th. After failing with Matt Wells and his 7-16 record in Big 12 play, which was as predictable at the time of hire as a West Texas dust storm, Athletic Director Kirby Hocutt went to a very different well to cool down his own steaming barcalounger. Eschewing outsiders, Hocutt made a hire focused on the state of Texas, more specifically the state's passion for Texas high school football. He went and got Joey McGuire. Texas Tech hired their version of Jeff Traylor at UTSA.

McGuire established his coaching legend at Cedar Hill high school in DFW, winning four state titles and using that job to catapult into the college ranks at Baylor under Matt Rhule. McGuire has only coached positions at the college level, but Tech is betting that he can bring his high school winning ways and overall program stewardship to Lubbock while taking advantage of his deep relationships with Texas high school coaches on the recruiting trail. Texas Tech is going all in on the state of Texas. Or are they? The Red Raiders may feature the most mercenary starting 22 in college football next year. 12 of their 22 starters will be former transfers and while working the portal will be crucial for the FBS middle class in the coming years, McGuire also needs to build out the infrastructure of the program with his own recruits. Having over half your team not particularly sure how the fight song goes is one of the strange guideposts of college football's new order.

McGuire, to his credit, did not hire in an insular fashion or seek to build out his staff with his old coaching buddies, retreads, or comfort hires. Texas Tech has a young and hungry staff (which includes former Longhorn Josh Cochran coaching tight ends) and he made two wise coordinator hires: up and coming offensive coordinator Zach Kittley and veteran defensive coordinator Tim DeRuyter. Kittley is the young architect of the Spread N Shred offense at Houston Baptist and Western Kentucky. Kittley took the best characteristics of the Air Raid (no huddle, tempo, simplicity) and married it to constant misdirection, screens, and deep balls. Everything builds off of everything else and it all looks the same formationally. Kittley spends 60 minutes every Saturday terrorizing poor safeties and linebackers who keep getting conflicting information on their responsibilities. He also got formerly unknown quarterback Bailey Zappe drafted in the 4th round by the New England Patriots. Zappe's 5967 yards passing and 62 touchdowns as a senior at Western Kentucky shattered the NCAA record books. Defensive coordinator Tim DeRuyter is an old, established defensive coordinator with stops at Oregon, Cal, A&M, Air Force and a head coaching run at Fresno State. He isn't a bright eyed and bushy tailed young riser, but he is a respected veteran who is very good at crafting defenses that disguise coverages, force turnovers, and disrupt offenses with superior talent. He is the perfect fit for the Red Raiders and where their current strengths rest. It is too early to know if Joey McGuire will succeed in Lubbock, but his offseason hires suggest a coach who is committed to breaking the Red Raiders out of their losing comfort zone.

Strengths

Texas Tech will boast one of the best secondaries in the Big 12, an assertion rarely made about a team that has traditionally struggled to find speed and reliable tacklers on the back end. Four Red Raiders defensive back starters have notched at least 20 starts in their careers and all five starters are seniors, most of them 5th or 6th year players. 2023 promises to be an adventure when everyone graduates, but for now Texas Tech will reap the benefits of having five starters who get senior citizen discounts at Luby's. Dadrion Taylor-Demerson is their best playmaking safety (3 interceptions, 10 pass break ups last year) and nickel Reggie Pearson, a transfer from Wisconsin, was solid last year and the talk of the offseason. Malik Dunlap and the perpetually eligible Adrian Frye, who first arrived at Tech during the latter part of the Carter presidency, round out the starting cornerbacks. At 6-0, 200 and 6-3, 215, they are the biggest, most physical corner combination in the league. Finally, big hitter

Marquis Watters (6-0, 215), a former transfer from Duke with 39 starts under his belt, rounds out the unit. He suffered a season ending injury against Texas last year, but he is back to full strength. Tech's secondary is huge, veteran, and a perfect fit for the kinds of disguised zone-man hybrid coverages and robber concepts that Tim DeRuyter loves to run. Expect the Red Raiders to engage in a great deal of coverage mischief.

Texas A&M transfer Tyree Wilson broke out last year for the Raiders, earning 7 sacks to go with his 13.5 tackles for loss. The imposing 6-6, 275 athlete has NFL potential and he will be the best player in the Texas Tech front six. He is a fine piece to build around and a likely 1st Team All-Big 12 performer.

If the Texas Tech starting tight ends don't get it done on the football field, head basketball coach Mark Adams may have a spot for them on the court. Mason Tharp is a huge 6-9 250 athlete who will certainly represent a red zone challenge, while former elite recruit Baylor Cupp, a transfer from Texas A&M, checks in at 6-7, 250. Cupp has seen his college career sidelined by constant injuries, but if healthy, he is a NFL level talent and a potential superstar. While Tech must replace the excellent NFL bound Erik Ezukanma at wide receiver, they have some solid prospects in slot Myles Price, big Loic Fouonji, and the even bigger JJ Sparkman. Given the confluence of talent and their offense, put your money on the Red Raider receiving corps being a pleasant surprise with breakout candidates across the board.

Tahj Brooks is a good runner and the skill player from Manor will be more prominently featured in 2022 if he can stay healthy. He averaged 6.5 yards per carry and scored 7 touchdowns last year. He will likely split time with SaRodorick Thompson, one of the lesser knights of Arthurian legend.

Weaknesses

The Texas Tech offensive line will need all of the help that it can get from Kittley's new misdirection offense. The genius of the scheme should take some of the pressure off of a unit breaking in three new starters, but other than established veteran guard Weston Wright and left tackle Caleb Rogers, the other three starters are marginal at best and the group will be suspect against higher end defensive lines. Speaking of defense, outside of Tyree Wilson and veteran linebacker Krishon Merriweather, the Texas Tech front six has some experienced players, but not a lot of playmakers. The replacement dropoff at linebacker from Colin Schooler and Riko Jeffers appears particularly drastic. Expect DeRuyter to mitigate that by staying in a base nickel.

Former Oregon Duck quarterback Tyler Shough looked good until he broke his collarbone against Texas in the fourth game of the season. The 6-5, 220 signal caller from Chandler, AZ has a big arm, an easy release, and certainly looks the polished part but he will be challenged for the starting job by Donovan Smith and young Behren Morton. The 6-5, 230 pound Smith was largely up to the task last year, finishing with a 146 passer rating while averaging 8.5 yards per attempt. He also exhibited above average running ability. Morton is a highly regarded recruit who has impressed in practice. The only reason Shough is not the obvious choice, or may not remain so a few games into the season, is that the new offense inordinately values quick decision making, accuracy, and recognition over gross physical traits. Offensive coordinator Zach Kittley wants a conduit, not an athlete trying to create. The conventional wisdom on Shough is that he uses terrific physical traits to compensate for mediocre game feel. Kittley would prefer those attributes in reverse.

Overview

Entering his 4th season in Morgantown, Neal Brown finds himself at a critical crossroads. Just 11-15 in Big 12 play since 2019, the Mountaineers are looking for their first winning league record during his tenure (WVU was .500 in 2020). Unfortunately they will face some headwinds in the hollers as the Mountaineers grapple with returning only 3 starters from a respectable 2021 defense that kept West Virginia in almost every game they played. That unit surrendered 23.8 points per game and 350 yards per contest despite receiving minimal help from a limited offense led by popgun armed quarterback Jarret Doege, but that potential source of strength was decimated after losing four prospective starters in the offseason portal, including All-Big 12 standout defensive lineman Akheem Mesidor. This is not the first time that Brown has seen an offseason portal exodus during his tenure and while early in the curve of cultural adoption it is understandable, probably healthy, losing respected starters four years in suggests that Brown and his staff are not adequately connecting with their players. West Virginia responded by inviting in their own portal mercenaries, as evidenced by a 2022 defense that will start seven former transfers, with three on offense for good measure. Brown is losing the portal wars and that presages losing too many battles on Saturday.

Brown will try to stem that tide with a revamped offensive staff led by new offensive coordinator Graham Harrell and transfer QB JT Daniels. Daniels was a prized national recruit who played at USC before transferring to Georgia and eventually losing the starting job to Stetson Bennett. Harrell will install his preferred Air Raid system and Daniels will parlay his experience (he has 19 career starts over four years, accumulating 4,840 yards passing, 32 touchdowns and 16 interceptions) and superior arm to create a potentially more dynamic offense. West Virginia had better score some points this year or Neal Brown is going to be searching the classified ads.

Strengths

The West Virginia offensive line, a significant team weakness for the last couple of years, may be finally coming into its own. The Mountaineers return all five starters and left tackle Wyatt Milum and center Zach Frazier will contend for all-conference honors. This is one of the more athletic units that West Virginia has fielded in some time, but they must improve unit cohesion as they surrendered 38 sacks last year and struggled to open consistent holes for departed leading rusher Leddie Brown. The sack number is concerning as JT Daniels is notably immobile and does not reliably sense pressure. If West Virginia is going to markedly improve a bottom tier offense, it will be because Daniels and the offensive line were able to create clean pockets and unleash his arm.

West Virginia's Casey Legg is the best kicker in the league. He was 19 of 23 on his attempts last year (82.6%) and was nails on several big kicks. A great kicker named Legg makes a lot of sense if you subscribe to the name-is-destiny school of Johnny Cash and a Boy Named Sue. Neal Brown should consider pursuing a quarterback named Joe Armm or a linebacker called Tyrone Hardhitz.

Senior Bryce Ford-Wheaton is poised for a big 2022. The talented 6-3, 220 pound receiver put up relatively modest numbers (42-575-3 tds) last year, but he will be the primary target of the passing game. Given Graham Harrell's penchant for 50+ attempt passing games, it is a good bet that Ford-Wheaton will see 10+ targets per game. Steady senior Sam James (20 starts) will be his complement. West Virginia's wide receiver corps is a qualified strength given their experience and above average ability. The real question to be answered is the degree to which Jarret Doege limited their ability to make plays downfield. JT Daniels, whatever his other faults, will help the Mountaineers answer that question early and often.

Dante Stills will return for his 5th year after brother Darius departed last year. When finishes the year and enters the NFL Draft, the Stills era will be over. They will be missed as it will prevent this preview from making moonshining jokes and Stills water runs deep quips, but Big 12 offensive linemen will not miss Dante Stills one bit. Stills has started 26 games during his career and amassed 19 career sacks to go with 43.5 tackles for loss. Leaner and bigger framed (6-4, 285) than his bowling ball brother, Dante has a great first step and can be lined up anywhere on the front and maintain his effectiveness. He must be the lynchpin of a denuded Mountaineer defense that will replace large swathes of experience and talent.

Weaknesses

West Virginia has hung their coonskin cap of respectability on their defense for three years running, but that likely ends this year. The Mountaineers lost too much on defense and the influx of seven starting transfers to stem the tide reeks more of desperation than a chance for upgrade. Outside of Dante Stills, there is no clear impact player and their new starting defense features transfers from South Dakota State, Illinois State, East Carolina, something called Jones College, and Murray State. There are very good players at the lower levels of college football looking for a spotlight, but are we to believe that West Virginia somehow found ALL OF THEM? This looks like it could all end quite terribly, in fact.

This preview has historically done a pretty good job of gauging the temperature on various coaching hot seats and making predictions about job risk, whether Les Miles at Kansas, Matt Wells at Texas Tech, Tom Herman and Charlie Strong at Texas, or surprising to many but this preview's readers, Gary Patterson at TCU. Neal Brown is currently checking all of the boxes for a coach who looks like he is about to get fired: massive offseason transfers from respected players, stories of internal unrest, a desperation offensive coordinator hire, an influx of warm body transfers from schools that no one knew existed, and a general prickly vibe about being challenged that West Virginia has not yet turned the corner. That all written, his teams are not following the pattern of a soon-to-be fired coach on the field of play. Quite simply, West Virginia plays really damn hard. And has done so for three years running. Brown has a scrappy football team. Does that continue? It must for Brown's sake. Because if West Virginia's Appalachian dawg mentality dissipates even one bit, this team has implosion potential.

Big XII Conference
Brent Venables | 1st season

Oklahoma Sooners

October 8 | Dallas, TX

2021 Record	3-yr Trend	5-yr Trend
11-2	32-6	56-10

Returning Starters	Offense	Defense
9	5	4

Overview

Well, the Oklahoma Sooners certainly had an interesting offseason.

They were utterly blindsided by their young head coach Lincoln Riley, who left Norman for the USC job. A coach who won five Big 12 titles in six years, secured six Top 10 finishes, went 5-1 against hated rival Texas, tutored two Heisman winners, went 55-10 overall, and is widely considered the finest offensive mind in college football. Wait, there is more…

After Spencer Rattler went up in flames, star quarterback Caleb Williams saved the season for OU, showing a bewitching combination of raw arm and running ability. Oklahoma had its star quarterback for at least the next two years! Except that Williams left with Riley and brought wide receiver Mario Williams with him. Promising backup cornerback Latrell McCutchin followed not long after. Wide-out Jadon Haselwood hit the bricks for his native Arkansas. Three year starting safety Patrick Fields fled to Stanford (no cultural adjustment there) and starting tight end Austin Stogner went to South Carolina. Spencer Rattler also became a Gamecock, but he always was one, wasn't he?

Oklahoma fans and administration descended into a frenzy of rage, grief, bargaining, denial, and scorn. How well did they handle it? The Oklahoma legislature passed a bill naming the westernmost 3 inches of highway leaving the state The Lincoln Riley Highway, an act of scorned impotence that made the 3 inch measurement work on several levels.

Anyway, that was the Sooner offseason. How was yours?

Oklahoma athletic director Joe Castiglione got up from the canvas and immediately hired Brent Venables, Clemson's star defensive coordinator. It was an attempt to recreate the magic of another former defensive coordinator hired to be head coach in Bob Stoops. Venables and Stoops, of course, had their own connection, having served as defensive coordinator for Coach Stoops at Oklahoma, eventually fleeing in 2012 when Bob attempted to force him into a co-defensive coordinator role with his incompetent brother Mike. Living well is the best revenge and Venables certainly did that at Clemson. That first meeting back with Bob was probably an interesting one. Venables hit the ground running, hired some new blood (Jeff Lebby from Ole Miss as offensive coordinator, old veteran defensive coordinator Ted Roof to lead the defense) and retained some old (Cale Gundy is still around), and worked the portal to Oklahoma's benefit despite taking major personnel losses. The Sooners return only 9 starters from the 2021 team that won six games by a touchdown or less. The media polls and prognosticators still see Sooner Magic, this preview says Venables won't pull a rabbit out of his hat.

Strengths

Former UCF quarterback Dillon Gabriel may not be the force of nature that former Sooner signal caller Caleb Williams is physically, but the veteran transfer is a proven team leader and a highly capable passer. He will also be reunited with Jeff Lebby, his old UCF offensive coordinator in 2019. The 5-11, 185 pound Hawaii native is an accurate, poised thrower who put up terrific numbers at UCF, totaling 8,037 passing yards, 70 touchdowns, and 14 interceptions over his career while demonstrating a nice deep ball touch that resulted in a hefty 14.5 yards per completion. Gabriel is mobile and elusive, but judicious as a runner, particularly after having his junior season ended at Louisville on the last play of the game with a broken clavicle. Oklahoma will run Gabriel a little, but he will not provide the game-changing rushing impact of his predecessor. Gabriel was a big get for the Sooners, who were effectively left high and dry by the Williams transfer. He has started 26 games in college and should have no problems adjusting to the game speed of the Big 12 in a familiar offense, however his slight stature and desire to extend plays could expose a woefully thin Sooner quarterback depth chart. If Gabriel goes down, the Sooner season goes down with him.

3 of the top 4 receiver targets for the Sooners from last year are gone, but the best of the bunch, swift Marvin Mims, is back. The elite deep threat (32 catches, 705 yards, over 22 yards a catch last year) should be a 1,000+ yard receiver this year and the primary focus of the Sooner passing attack. H-back Brayden Willis is an underrated piece in the Sooner offense and he should see his passing targets double in 2022. However, Oklahoma's tradition of outstanding blockers at fullback and H-back, key

to the running game under Lincoln Riley, is over. That is something to be mindful of when assessing their larger scheme. The Sooners are also hoping that former elite recruit Theo Wease finally lives up to his billing at wideout. Drake Stoops will be a sure-handed option in the slot. Arizona State transfer LV Bunkley-Shelton had 33 catches for the Sun Devils last year and he should also bring some juice. Overall, the Sooner passing game has their elite target and a strong enough supporting cast to realize the vision of what Jeff Lebby wants to do on offense in the passing game, but a traditionally dominant Sooner rushing attack will have some major schematic and personnel headwinds in 2022.

Weaknesses

Oklahoma's defense did not live up to the hype last year, finishing 56th in the nation by advanced metrics. They also lost all of their most impactful players to the NFL draft: edge rusher Nik Bonitto, nose tackle Perrion Winfrey, defensive end Isaiah Thomas, safety Delarrin Turner Yell, and leading tackler inside linebacker Brian Asamoah. Those not lost to the draft were lost to the portal: safety Patrick Fields took his nearly 40 career starts to Stanford. They even lost an underrated depth piece at defensive end in speedy LaRon Stokes, who would have been a fine extra year senior. While good players like Jalen Redmond, Marcus Stripling and Dashaun White return, the three best Sooner pass rushers are gone along with a ton of talent, productivity, and experience from the second and third levels. The sum was less than the parts last year and they managed to lose all of the best parts. Nor does Brent Venables inherit a roster of defensive linemen or defensive backs that suit his preferences. Yet national pundits and prognosticators still pick Oklahoma for the Big 12 title out of laziness, or perhaps sheer force of habit. The idea that the Sooner defense "should be fine, because Venables knows defense" is more astrology than science. Why will Oklahoma be fine? Because they have paper clips on their helmets? College football fans and media are engaged in a giant case of normalcy bias. Oklahoma has been good and wins the Big 12 for as long as they can remember, so they will do so again. They are looking at the showroom model and not lifting up the hood to reveal a very different engine. Brent Venables is one heck of a defensive mind and he will gather the pieces he needs soon enough, but he will have his hands full trying to field a good defense in 2022.

The Sooner offensive line took a major step back last year (33 sacks allowed) and the two primary drivers of the Sooner running game – home run running back Kennedy Brooks and dual threat monster Caleb Williams – are gone. Along with their departure goes the misdirection, deception, and quarterback running threat that saved the Sooner bacon last year in several close games. Offensive line guru Bill Bedenbaugh is a master of his craft and he has bright spots in Cal transfer McKade

Mettauer and left tackle Anton Harrison, but the rest of the unit does not inspire after losing their only truly physical guy in NFL draft pick Marquis Hayes. Right tackle Wanya Morris has 5 star pedigree, but that has not yet shown up on the field and guard Chris Murray and center Andrew Raym struggle with tough interior defenders. Bedenbaugh will wring improved play out of his charges if it kills him…or them…but he only has so many miracles in his whistle. The dominant Sooner offensive linemen that characterized and defined their most explosive offenses are simply not there anymore. Without the run threat of Caleb Williams, how will Oklahoma create a consistent ground game? Expect an offense buoyed by Williams and Brooks that ran for a healthy 5.4 yards per attempt last year to dip below 5 yards per attempt over the course of the season.

Big XII Conference
Matt Campbell | 8th season

Iowa State Cyclones

October 15 | Austin TX

2021 Record	3-yr Trend	5-yr Trend
7-6	23-15	39-15

Returning Starters	Offense	Defense
8	5	3

Overview

Remember when 2021 was built up as the year that the Iowa State Cyclones would field the best team in program history? The Cyclones were going to storm through the Big 12, an unforgiving wind that would decimate Oklahoma flatland trailers and Texas penthouses with indifferent cruelty. They would strip Baylor's khakis down to their tighty whities and reduce West Virginia's finest outhouses to the studs. The time of Iowan hegemony had arrived! Every preseason publication named them a Top 10 team. For good reason. They returned 19 starters, a 4th year veteran quarterback that was being touted as a potential 1st round pick, a loaded defense, NFL tight ends, receivers, and running backs and a well-respected, overachieving young coach that college football powers have been sending feelers to for three years running. What's not to love? A teenager who coats his face in motor oil before he goes to bed could not be a more obvious breakout candidate. Yeah, about that. It didn't quite pan out. It turns out that a football is shaped funny, tends to bounce weird, and predicting the performance of a 20 year old every Saturday is not exactly science. As the great screenwriter William Goldman once remarked: "No one knows anything." Not exactly the best marketing tact for a college football preview to offer its readers, but there you go.

The Cyclones went 7-6 (5-4 in Big 12 play) for their 5th consecutive winning season under Matt Campbell, but that was little solace for a Cyclone fan base indulging fanciful dreams of the college football playoff. Media did quite a bit to promote that expectation and this preview may have even slated the Cyclones for a 9-3 or 10-2 regular season. Instead, Iowa State went 1-5 in games decided by a touchdown or less. It happens. Wins and losses are binary and close only counts in horseshoes, hand grenades, and airplane body odor. Run the season back again ten times and the Cyclones probably average 9 wins, but win expectancy is played out in one season, not in the mean or median of a million computer simulations. Brock Purdy was not great, the Iowa State offense seemed to run out of ideas, and the Cyclones demonstrated a consistent knack for losing close games.

Iowa State fans grumbling about Matt Campbell need to stop guzzling ethanol. The Iowa State Cyclone have won nine games exactly three times in their entire program history. In 1906, 2000, and in 2020. We all remember that 1906 team fondly. No one will soon forget their riveting games with Coe, Grinnell, and Morningside. Those were some of their actual opponents and instead of helmets, the players wore wreaths made of corn stalks. The losing team volunteered five men with gumption to be ritually sacrificed with a threshing scythe and their grieving widows received a bag of nickels and a warm handshake from President Theodore Roosevelt. Those were simpler times, and in many ways better. The point of that digression is this: Iowa State was 8-28 the three years before Matt Campbell arrived on campus. The program boasts a losing record over its lifetime. They did not have a single winning season in the entire 1990s. They have gone 39-25 over the last five seasons, have a respected program, and last year excepted, tend to play over their heads every Saturday. While this is clearly a rebuilding year, no one should underestimate Campbell's ability to build an infrastructure quickly and find a way to win games. As for the larger question of whether Campbell has maximized his career path in Ames, the answer is a clear yes. Unless he is satisfied with his current lot, he may want to start looking at his upward options before a run of bad program luck robs him of the chance to climb the ladder while his name is still hot. No Big 12 program returns fewer starters than Iowa State's eight and they lost four players to the NFL draft. The last time Iowa State did that was in 1977.

Strengths

The Iowa State offensive line boasts a strong, experienced lineup from center to right tackle with Trevor Downing, Darrell Simmons, and Jake Remsburg. Though the left side is a bit more iffy, the overall unit is strong and Downing's move to center should be a stabilizing force for them overall. They will put as many as three offensive linemen on postseason All-Big 12 teams and will form a solid base from which to rebuild a skill group that was largely leveled by graduation. If the Iowa State offense exceeds expectations, it will be because this unit and new quarterback Hunter Dekkers came up big.

The Cyclones have three individual performers deserving specific mention: receiver Xavier Hutchinson, defensive end Will McDonald, and safety Anthony Johnson. Xavier Hutchinson grew into his own last year, grabbing 82 balls for just under 1,000 yards and 5 touchdowns. He is the best possession receiver in the Big 12 and he does a great job using his 6-3, 210 pound frame and quality hands to create easy windows for his quarterback. The Cyclones lost both starting tight ends and oft-injured

Tariq Milton to the Texas Longhorns and will count heavily on Hutchinson to carry the load until they can find secondary and tertiary receiving options. Anthony Johnson has started an amazing 42 games in his Cyclone career, most of them at cornerback. Heacock moved him to safety to fill an enormous gap of experience and talent and the 6-0, 200 pound veteran should excel there. Johnson is a physical tackler with above average pure coverage skills and they will count on him to improve a young secondary that will struggle to match last year's unit that led the league in passing efficiency defense. Finally, Will McDonald is the best pure talent returning on the Cyclone defense. The 6-4, 245 pound cat quick edge rusher has added good weight to a frame that used to carry just 200 pounds and last year he notched 11.5 sacks to go with 5 forced fumbles. McDonald was not a one year wonder. In 2019, he nabbed 6 sacks in limited action and the following year he secured another 10.5. He is the most proven and talented pure pass rusher in the league. That written, he was a part of a larger defense that did an excellent job of hunting positive matchups for him with a stunting linebacker corps and fellow defensive linemen who could exploit one on one matchups. McDonald should be very good again, but teams should be able to game plan him in ways they could not last year.

Weaknesses

Iowa State turns a new page in their offensive backfield and loses a coterie of chain moving tight ends. Rugged sophomore Hunter Dekkers takes over at quarterback, ending the four year reign of Brock Purdy. Purdy was inconsistent at times last year, but he has been a productive fixture in Ames and the best quarterback that Campbell has had during his tenure. Dekkers will be asked to spark an offense that grew stale and his legs will play a prominent role in that. Dekkers is a strong, tough athlete (6-3, 235) and a very capable runner. Expect the Cyclones to install some quarterback run game to exploit his power and running ability to help open up Campbell's offense. Dekkers got some game repetitions last year and Iowa State observers are optimistic about his passing ability, but the rubber meets the road on game day. Iowa State also lost home running back Breece Hall. Hall had nearly 1500 yards rushing last year and his 5.8 yards per carry average revealed his penchant for big runs. He will be replaced by Jirehl Brock, who boasts similar size to Hall, but perhaps not as much finishing speed. He saw limited action last year gaining 174 yards rushing, but it will be his job this fall. Tight end Charlie Kolar's departure to the NFL will leave a gaping hole in production and remove a valuable chain mover and red zone threat. Kolar and fellow departed tight end Chase Allen combined for 88 catches and 8 touchdowns last year. Easton Dean and Jared Rus will try to replace them, but Iowa State will have to place an enormous passing game burden on Xavier Hutchinson.

Iowa State's borderline elite defense last year was wrecked by graduation and transfer. They lose most of their defensive line, the best all-around linebacker in the Big 12 in Mike Rose, and a good portion of their secondary. Discouragingly, a pair of likely starters – Isheem Young and Datrone Young – who could have offered some stability during their transition year, transferred to Ole Miss and Duke, respectively. The Iowa State defense is starting over and while they are extremely well coached by veteran Jon Heacock, a lot of their schematic success depends on cohesion and experience at safety and linebacker. That is gone and it is going to take time for it to develop. Expect the Cyclones to take a significant step back from last year's 11th ranked national defense. Heacock and the program infrastructure will not allow them to fall past 50th, but that is a massive delta of performance for a team that will also be breaking in a new offense. The teams that face Iowa State in September and October are going to be glad that they did.

Overview

The Cowboys and Mike Gundy smashed preseason expectations of a rebuilding year by going 12-2, beating hated big brother Oklahoma, taking down Texas in Austin, falling a few inches short of a Big 12 title, and ended the year upsetting Notre Dame in a thrilling bowl game. Perhaps surprisingly, they once again did it with a terrific all-around defense that finished the season ranked 5th nationally by advanced metrics. In 2020, the Cowboys were ranked 14th nationally, but defensive coordinator Jim Knowles put together a masterpiece in his final season in Stillwater. The Cowboys seemed to get key development at every position required and the coaching performance put in by the staff was nothing short of elite. Underestimating a grown man over age 40 rarely pays off. Mike Gundy, the man, the mullet, the legend. The greatest coach in Cowboy football history has ignored the clarion call of other programs, either due to general contentment, loyalty to his alma mater, or perhaps an understanding that he has carved out the perfect niche of coaching a well-resourced, respected program where expectations are still measured and fans can still remember the dark days before his arrival in 2005. Gundy boasts a terrific 149-69 record in Stillwater, his only losing season was his first, and the Cowboys have finished nationally ranked in 5 of his last 7 seasons and 9 times overall. Texas fans would take performance over the last decade in a heartbeat.

Expectations for 2022 are mixed, though no one is underestimating the Cowboys. The defense will have to weather some tough losses, but they return the best defensive line in the conference. They will miss Jim Knowles, but Derek Mason is a well-regarded replacement. Offensively, they will have to once again surmount a middling at best offensive line, but Gundy and his offensive brain trust have been maximizers on that side of the ball for nearly two decades.

Strengths

Quarterback Spencer Sanders returns and how you feel about that fact tells you all you need to know about this quarterbacking rorschach test. Some people see a beautiful butterfly, others see a man throwing an interception into triple coverage off of his back foot. In three years as a starter, Sanders has thrown 31 interceptions and a heck of a lot of them are of the hair ripping variety. Why does Gundy put up with it? For one, a lack of better options. Two? Because when Sanders is on, he can be electric. In the bowl game against Notre Dame, Sanders looked like the best player on the field. He ran for 125 yards on 17 carries and threw for another 371 yards and four touchdown passes with zero interceptions. His 496 yards of offense led the Cowboys to victory in an all-time performance. It was not the first time he has come up big in the spotlight in a bowl game. The prior year, he threw for 300+ yards and four touchdowns against the Miami Hurricanes. How do you square that with the passer who threw 7 interceptions against Baylor in two games? Or went 6 of 13 for 82 yards on the road against Boise State? Or averaged a modest 7.2 yards per passing attempt for the season? If we knew that, we would tell Mike Gundy and earn a fat consulting fee. However, the basic rule of thumb for Sanders is that teams who can keep him in the pocket and force him off of his spots and muddy upf his first read, tend to have a lot of success against him. Success of the "Is Sanders betting on the game against the Cowboys?" variety. However, when Sanders starts running around to free up wide receivers downfield, grabs big chunk gains on scrambles, and generally starts to feel it, batten down the defensive hatches because his momentum gets difficult to derail. As often as Oklahoma State relied on Spencer Sanders to win games, they also minimized and protected him in some key situations. Whether Sanders is the best hope for the Cowboys winning the league or whether he is the player that will hold them back from their ultimate success is in the eye of the beholder. Sanders Law of Equilibrium states that he will provide persuasive evidence for his fans and detractors equally over enough Saturdays.

The Oklahoma State defensive front is fantastic. They are deep, physical, technically sound, and well conditioned. Big strongside defensive end Tyler Lacy (6-4, 295) is a fine run stopper with just enough athletic ability to create pass rush and disruption. He can also shift inside when Oklahoma State wants to play their best pass rushing combo. Lacy totalled 3.5 sacks and 11.5 tackles for loss last year. Overachieving Brock Martin brought heat at the other end, totaling 9 sacks and 14 tackles for loss of his own. Martin just has a knack for getting the passer. Undersized Collin Oliver (6-2, 225) complements the edge group with the best pass rushing skill set on the team. He had 10.5 sacks playing 35 snaps a game. The feast of edge play continues with Trace Ford (a former starter recovering from his second ACL tear) and Kody Walterscheid. Inside, the Cowboys rely on big Sione Asi to jam up the interior and Brendon Evers is the penetrating 3 technique. Evers notched 3 sacks and 6 tackles for loss in limited snaps last year and the staff expect big things from the 6-2, 295 pound penetrator. Any offensive line that cannot handle the Cowboy front is going to have a long day at the office. They are deep, talented, and come at opponents in waves.

Though Oklahoma State loses #1 receiver Tay Martin to graduation (he had 80 catches and over 1,000 yards receiving and 10 touchdowns last year) they return 7 of their top 8 pass catchers and Oklahoma State coaches are quietly confident in the talent level they have, if relatively unproven. Look for Brennan Presley, Jaden Bray, Rashod Owens and Braydon Johnson to form one of the better receiving corps in the league by year end. Oklahoma State's historical knack for developing the position and locating athletic marvels who somehow flew under the recruiting radar is time proven. They will do it again in 2022.

Weaknesses

The losses on the Cowboy 2nd level and back end are pretty devastating. They lose their top 4 tacklers from last year, including clutch linebacker Malcolm Rodriguez, who led the team in tackles, as well as key blitzer and fellow linebacker Devin Harper who was second in tackles and incredibly disruptive. Both were drafted by the NFL. The Cowboys also lost four of their five starters in the secondary, a unit that keyed an underrated pass defense. Three year starting cornerback and All-Big 12 performer Jarrick Bernard-Converse using an extra year of eligibility to play his final season at LSU is a particularly bad beat. The sole returnee, Jason Taylor, who Texas fans may remember from a Casey Thompson pick six, is a very good player, but he will need to lead a group of unproven newbies. Cornerbacks Jabbar Muhammad and Korie Black have seen game action but are still largely untested. High level cornerback play was a key element of Cowboy defensive success over the last two seasons and it stands to reason that this unit will take a step back. If the Cowboy defensive line does not do its work early, the Cowboys will feature a vulnerable secondary.

The offensive line is not very good. They were not very good last year and still made chicken salad out of chicken droppings, but credit the hard running of departed Jaylan Warren and a quick timing-oriented Cowboy passing game for covering up their sins. Opponents only notched 17 sacks against the unit, causing some media who scan box scores for their takes to pronounce the unit sound, but game film showed a very different reality. The upside of the group rests heavily on former JUCO right tackle Caleb Etienne, a 6-7, 325 monster who has thus far looked better in pads than on the field, and undersized left tackle Tyrone Webber (6-3, 285). If both step up, the Cowboys offense has a real shot at evolving from a simplistic and predictable scheme built around quarterback preservation into a bolder downfield offense that could unlock Spencer Sanders more fully. Whether one wishes to fully unlock Spencer Sanders may be the larger question.

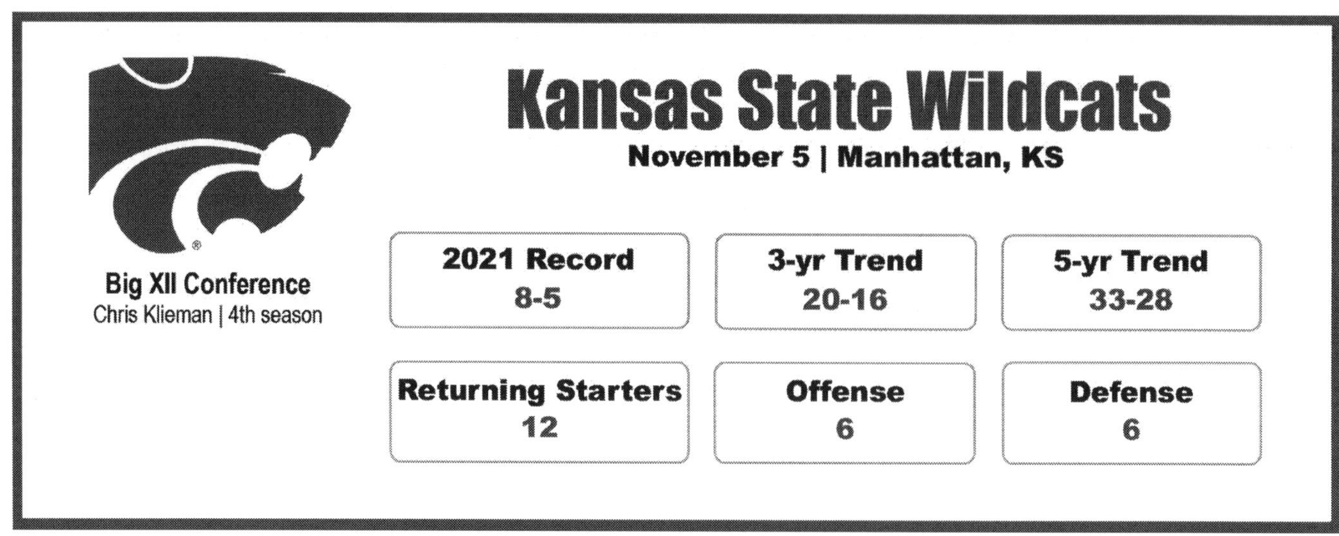

Overview

Chris Klieman is doing a good job in Manhattan, Kansas. Heading into this 4th season, he already boasts a winning record (20-16) and has taken a program that had relied too heavily on mercenaries and transfers and transformed it into a grow-your-own culture that uses the portal judiciously (as in securing new quarterback Adrian Martinez) while somehow not losing a single player in the offseason. Perhaps that is one of the advantages of not having many airline routes that fly into rural Kansas. It helps you keep your desirable players. Last season, the Wildcats were terrific against non-conference opponents, going a perfect 4-0 against the likes of LSU, Nevada and Stanford, but struggled to defeat the more talented teams in the Big 12, finishing with an overall 4-5 record in league play. Injuries to quarterback Skylar Thompson played a significant role in that, but more often than not, the Wildcats ran into a simple talent disparity against the league's upper echelon when injuries and exhaustion sapped a solid starting 22 that was backed up by a less than solid group of backups. Klieman needs more time to build out his program depth, but in the meanwhile if you are looking for a wildcard conference contender with some nice Vegas odds, the Cats are worth kicking the tires on. Of course, that requires a lot of things going their way, but at the very least the Wildcats will have an interesting enough roster composition and play just enough contrarian football that they will be a matchup nightmare for several "better" teams in the league.

Strengths

Skylar Thompson leaves as one of the most underappreciated players in Big 12 history, though Miami Dolphins scouts appreciated him enough to draft him. Thompson will be replaced by a transfer quarterback that few Nebraska fans have much appreciation for in quarterback Adrian Martinez. Martinez holds a dozen spots at the top of the Cornhusker record books, started 39 games over four years, has thrown for 8491 yards, rushed for 2301 yards (including four 500+ yard rushing seasons) and has accounted for a combined 80 touchdowns (45 passing, 35 rushing). So why were so many Big Red fans alright with seeing their 6-2, 220 pound quarterback go? Probably because he presided over one of the worst four year stretches in Cornhusker history. Nebraska went 15-29 over his four years in Lincoln, including an atrocious 10-25 Big 10 record. Mind you, Nebraska plays in the same Big 10 West division as Northwestern, Purdue, Minnesota, and Illinois! Was Martinez the talented hard luck hero trying to stem the tide of losing in a moribund program or was Martinez was one of the causal elements of that losing? Like Spencer Sanders at Oklahoma State, there is evidence for both the pro and con view. What is very clear is that Nebraska had much bigger problems than Adrian Martinez's play every weekend. A quarterback will always get too much credit in good times and too much blame in bad. Martinez will also get significantly better coaching. Klieman is terrific at fashioning game plans that a quarterback can do rather than whining about what his signal caller cannot and Kansas State will exploit Martinez's wheels in combination with Deuce Vaughn, create a lot of easy passing reads through the play action game, and disseminate the playmaking to a good wide receiver and running back group rather than place the outcome of the game on Martinez's shoulders every weekend. At the risk of oversimplification, if Martinez plays really well, Kansas State is a league title contender and will be a very dangerous team. If he is the same guy we saw in Lincoln, Kansas State will remain a respectable team that struggles to handle the conference elite.

Deuce Vaughn continues to be a revelation. The 5-5, 170 pound scatback has unnatural agility and quickness, consistently making very good athletes look foolish when they try to tackle him in the open field. He's also surprisingly durable, no longer consigned to being the change of pace option who cannot carry the mail for four quarters. Vaughn was a highlight reel performer all season, totaling 1404 yards rushing at 6.0 yards per carry while adding another 49 catches for 468 yards in the passing game. The diminutive speedster is tough as nails and held up to a brutal workload all season. He had 284 touches last year and should match that total again. Vaughn is one of the best two running backs in the Big 12 (perhaps you can guess the other?) and a must-watch performer on Saturday.

Kansas State has better receiving options than most casual fans know. The explosive Malik Knowles has real game-breaking potential and is an outstanding kick returner (he averaged 30 yards per return and brought two kicks back to the house last year) who is still learning to channel his speed into route-running. He caught 29 balls for 441 yards and 4 touchdowns last year and that total will grow. He is also a dangerous runner who should see plenty of work on jet sweeps and reverses. Polished Philip Brooks also returns and he added 43 catches last year for 543 yards. Possession receiver

Chabastin Taylor rounds out the group and the fly-paper handed 6-4, 225 pounder is almost two years out from the knee injury that hampered his play in 2021.

The Wildcats boast several high level performers on every level of their defense, most of which seem to fly under the popular media radar. Eli Huggins holds down the fort at nose tackle and is a solid run stopper but the real star upfront is Felix Anudike-Uzomah. The 255 pound defensive end is a top notch pass rusher who totaled 11 sacks last year while forcing an amazing 6 fumbles. He is a difference maker who is only getting better. Behind him is one of the most quietly effective linebackers in the league in Daniel Green. Green is a plus athlete and big hitter who led the Wildcats in tackles with 89 while adding 16 tackles for loss and 3 sacks. Transfer Will Honas is finally healthy and Wildcat coaches are excited to see the savvy Honas suit up for his final season. Kansas State also has a pair of proven cornerbacks in big press corner Julius Brents (6-4, 205) and Ekow Boye-Doe. Brents is huge and a potential NFL prospect. Boye-Doe is not a doughboy at a slender 6-0, 170, but the 5th year senior is quality in pass coverage, though he can be exploited in the run game. If the Wildcats have a weakness on defense, it is a lack of size on their defensive line and the need to break in an entirely new group of safeties. Big 12 teams that can go big and get physical on offense and play action deep off of that will give them problems, but the pass-happy teams in the league will have their hands full with the Wildcat pass rush and cornerback play. Particularly if the Wildcat offense can successfully ball control them on the other end.

Weaknesses

Kansas State lost three interior offensive line starters. The Cats are historically pretty good at replacing offensive linemen, but the general trend is for those replacements to struggle against highly physical interior defensive lines in their first year. The Cats will lean heavily on left tackle Cooper Beebe to stabilize the line and keep Martinez cleaner than a preacher's alibi in a liquor store parking lot.

While deliberate pace and calculation are key elements of the Wildcat contrarian style and they averaged an excellent 6.3 yards per play despite averaging only 363 yards per game of total offense, the offense struggled to score much against the league's best and averaged only 28 points per game overall. Don't expect Chris Klieman to go to a four wide hurry up base offense, but given the speed and quickness in the Cat backfield and on the perimeter, in combination with Martinez's legs and experience, it may not be the worst idea to eschew deliberation from time to time and see what the offense can do going fast.

Big XII Conference
Sonny Dykes | 1st season

TCU Horned Frogs

November 12 | Austin, TX

2021 Record	3-yr Trend	5-yr Trend
5-7	16-18	34-27

Returning Starters	Offense	Defense
13	6	7

Overview

This preview has been hinting for years – at first softly, then moving to bludgeoning the reader – at the unthinkable: that Gary Patterson's time in Fort Worth was coming to an end. Texas fans never noticed discontent and the signs since the Frogs have managed to beat Texas more years than not of late (Patterson won 7 of the last 10) and fans tend to limit their universe in assessing a coach's fortunes based on how he performs against their team. TCU has not been a particularly good football team for some time now. Over the last six years they went 26-28 in Big 12 play and have had a sub .500 conference record in 66.7% of those seasons. Yes, it's true that Gary Patterson belongs in the College Football Hall of Fame and his 181-80 career record at a private school in Fort Worth speaks for itself, but the writing has been on the wall for some time. The only folks shocked that TCU let Patterson go – a victim of the very expectations that he himself created – were those not paying attention to the sure signs of a program drifting towards complacency and a singularly focused head coach who had the audacity to develop interests beyond football.

Now, if the preview was really good, it would have predicted that an embittered Patterson would take a consulting job at Texas, renewed, red-assed, and ready for revenge, looking to unlock a football program that has lacked the edge and attention to details needed to win big. Gary Patterson now has the enviable job of observing and advising without the stress and duress of having to call all of the shots, a consigliere with no risk of jail time or a rival hit. TCU has moved on, even if the Patterson statue – with stigmata of armpit and ass sweat on gameday – in front of their stadium cannot. Hiring head coach Sonny Dykes from SMU was the obvious hire, but was it the most forward looking? Dykes is a likable fellow with a good offensive mind, but three good years at SMU (25-10 record) terrorizing the likes of Abilene Christian, North Texas, Louisiana Tech, and Tulsa does not obscure a career 46-53 head coaching record at his other stops. Dykes hired Garrett Riley (younger brother of Lincoln) as his offensive coordinator and Joe Gillespie (formerly of Tulsa) as his defensive coordinator. The approachable and offensive minded Dykes feels like a classic oversteer from the contentious, defensive guru Patterson, but Dykes is a good recruiter with excellent connections in the DFW metroplex. Time will tell in Fort Worth if Dykes works out or not, but the 2022 season may prove to be a challenging one.

Strengths

Wide receiver Quentin Johnston is an absolute stud and the failure to get him the ball more than his 33 catches for 634 yards and 6 touchdowns last year was more a reflection of TCU's focus than Johnston. The Frogs discovered him late in the season hiding in plain sight and he topped 100 yards in three of his last five games. TCU's passing game will run through the 6-4, 200 pound explosive deep ball threat. Taye Barber is a solid complement to Johnston doing the dirty work underneath and Derius Davis has a bright future. Speedster Quincy Brown is one to keep an eye on as well. This is one of the better units in a league with wide receiver rooms that range from above average to outstanding. The degree to which they will be maximally exploited will depend on how the TCU starting quarterback battle resolves itself.

Cornerback Tre'vius Hodges-Tomlinson came out of nowhere to become the best lockdown cornerback in the Big 12 in 2020. Pro Football Focus named him a 1st Team All-American, he was named 1st Team All Big 12 by every organization, and also named to the 2nd Team All-American AP team. In 2021, Hodges-Tomlinson was largely avoided by opposing offenses, but repeated as a 1st Team All-Big 12 selection for the second year in a row. Tomlinson may have also fallen off a bit as the entire TCU defense broke down around him, but he still led the team in interceptions (2) and had seven pass break ups. He surrendered a single touchdown pass all season, which is remarkable given how forgiving the defense was around him. The Waco product is a small corner (5-9, 180) but he has good play strength and incredible recovery quickness. The solution to dealing with Hodges-Tomlinson is fairly straightforward: avoid and throw at the vulnerable personnel around him.

Weaknesses

The letter D has always been revered at Amon-Carter stadium when it comes to the TCU defense, but last year it stood for disaster. The Frogs finished 84th nationally by advanced metrics and it looked even worse than that on the field. They surrendered 463 yards per game, opponents averaged 34.9 points per contest, and they surrendered a mind blowing 7.2 yards per play. They bled big play after big play and they showed some quit late in the season. They could not stop the run (Oklahoma State ran for 8 touchdowns in a 63-17 laugh fest) and were helpless against the pass, despite the presence of a premier lockdown cornerback. They also had real trouble getting to the passer (only 15 sacks on the season) and then promptly lost their two best pass rushers to the portal in edge players Ochuan Mathis and Khari Coleman. The TCU defense returns linebacker Dee Winters to help stabilize the unit, but this bunch projects to be well below average.

There is a quarterback competition in Fort Worth. You would not know it from reading popular media or listening to press conferences, but Air Raid disciple Sonny Dykes wants to throw the football around to a talented Frog wide receiver group. That has not always been returning starter Max Duggan's wheelhouse. Duggan looked great statistically last year, notching a 157.6 passing efficiency rating, and showed a lot of improvement while battling through nagging injuries, but Chandler Morris showed natural passing instincts in his game action, which included a shocking upset of the Baylor Bears where Morris threw for 461 yards. Duggan is the superior runner, a tough team leader, and has 29 career starts under his belt, but Dykes is going to go with the quarterback who lets him run the offense that he wants to run.

Gary Patterson built a strong developmental culture at TCU predicated on patient long term development and a football first mentality, but a falloff on the field and on the recruiting trail forced him into taking some high profile transfers with checkered histories and less than team-first attitudes, forcing a critical breaking point where the culture no longer influenced the outliers, but the outliers started influencing the culture. Last year, the preview asked a provocative question: was TCU sitting on a knucklehead time bomb? The 2021 season answered with a resounding BOOM. Does the laid back Sonny Dykes have the ability to excise the cultural problems (talented running back Zach Evans has already portaled to Ole Miss) and get TCU back to a scrappy team first mentality? Absolutely...but not right away

Big XII Conference
Lance Leipold | 2nd season

Kansas Jayhawks

November 19 | Lawrence, KS

2021 Record	3-yr Trend	5-yr Trend
2-10	5-28	9-48

Returning Starters	Offense	Defense
17	9	8

Overview

Lance Leipold had a terrific run at Division III Wisconsin-Whitewater (is it a school, is it a rafting trip brochure) where he went 109-6 with six national championships. He then coached Buffalo to football relevance in the MAC conference going 37-33 over six years, twice earning MAC Coach of the Year honors. Leipold is a real honest-to-goodness football coach and that started to show late last year as the Jayhawks upset Texas, played Oklahoma, TCU and West Virginia close and generally looked like a FBS football team. A really bad FBS football team, but one that actually is competitive. Since 2011, Kansas has gone 20-100, but the 2021 Jayhawks were certainly better than their dismal 0-9 effort in 2020 under the bloated disgrace of a program led by Les Miles.

About that Texas loss. Hats off to Kansas for a spirited effort, but it was a pathetic display by the Longhorns, made even more humiliating by the fact that Texas has now lost twice in the last five years to the Jayhawks. Over that same time period, Kansas only won seven other games total! Kansas led 35-14 at halftime against a Texas team going through the motions and then withstood a furious second half rally, eventually winning in overtime on a touchdown followed by a two point conversion. Devin Neal ran for 143 yards on 24 carries and 3 touchdowns while poised quarterback Jadon Daniels totaled an error free 247 yards of offense rushing and passing while accounting for four touchdowns himself. The Jayhawks treated Pete Kwiatkowski's defense like a turnstile for most of the game but the offense was not without fault. The Longhorn offense racked up yardage and points, but they also committed four awful turnovers, including a pick 6 right before the end of the first half courtesy of Hudson Card. Burn the game film and pray that this was the low point of the Steve Sarkisian era. As for Kansas? A win to build on as they begin their long, slow incremental climb from the basement of college football.

Strengths

Kansas found a quarterback last year in Jadon Daniels. They tried Jason Bean and Miles Kendrick before settling on Daniels. Count on the Jayhawks to do the right thing after exhausting all other options. In limited action, Daniels threw for 860 yards, 7 touchdowns and 3 interceptions while rushing for another 3 touchdowns, but most of all he showed heart, drive, and competitiveness. Right now Lance Leipold isn't looking for superstars. He is looking for competitors and football players who will go out and fight, irrespective of the odds. That describes the 6-0, 215 pound Daniels and that is why he will be their quarterback in 2022.

The Jayhawks also found a running back in freshman Devin Neal. He rushed for 707 yards and 8 touchdowns at 4.5 yards per clip. Now a sophomore, Neal is a strong no-frills runner who gets his 215 pounds up the field as quickly as possible while not shying away from contact. His statistics were not eye popping due to a less than impressive supporting cast, but he came on late and is a natural tackle breaker. Neal will be joined by talented transfer Ky Thomas from Minnesota, who led the Gophers in rushing last year with 826 rushing yards and 149 yards in their bowl game win over West Virginia. They should be an effective 1-2 punch, particularly if the Jayhawk offensive line can ever get squared away. That unit does return four starters.

Safety Kenny Logan is the best player on the Kansas defense and one of the best defenders in the Big 12. He led the team in tackles with 113 stops, had an interception, forced two fumbles and also averaged 28 yards per return as a kickoff returner. The 210 pound athlete would start anywhere in the league and he will certainly draw NFL Draft scrutiny. Joining Logan is an interesting transfer, Miami of Ohio pass rusher Lonnie Phelps. Phelps totaled 9.5 sacks last year while earning 1st team All-MAC honors and will be a Day 1 starter on the edge. If he can bring a pass rush while linebackers Rich Miller and Gavin Potter stop the bleeding in the running game, Kansas has a shot at fielding a defense that is not execrable.

Weaknesses

The Jayhawks were brutal on defense last year, finishing 120th out of 130 FBS teams in efficiency defense. They allowed 42 points per game and conceded an ungodly 7.2 yards per play to their opponents. They struggled in all phases but exhibited almost no ability to stop the run, conceding 6 yards per carry and 40 rushing touchdowns on the season. Texas and the South Dakota Coyotes were the only teams on their schedule that did not exceed 200 yards rushing against them. Their only two wins of the season.

The Jayhawk offense did not exactly set the world on fire either, but finishing 76th nationally by advanced metrics is more palatable than their 84th ranked finish in 2020. Baby steps! If you are hunting for positives, the Jayhawks did a relatively good job of taking care of the football and their conservative, quick release passing offense did not expose their offensive line and that kept sack totals down. They also had very few penalties. Why the subpar performance overall then? A lack of explosive plays. Until Kansas gets more juice at the skill positions and better displacement from their offensive line, they will struggle to put points on the board consistently. Money downs were a consistent thorn in their wing. The Jayhawks converted 35% of their 3rd downs and opponents managed 54%. That 19 spread signals big trouble for any football team. They also converted nearly 37% on 4th downs, but the defense allowed a 61% conversion rate. A 24 point negative differential is not going to work. If they can ever cut the delta between those numbers to single digits, they will have a shot at winning four or five football games and rise from their seemingly perpetual spot in the league's cellar.

Overview

Two years ago, the preview accurately predicted that Baylor would crash back down to earth in 2020 after their brief ascendance under former head coach Matt Rhule. That they did, plummeting from a 11-3 record to a 2-7 debacle under rookie head coach Dave Aranda in a lockdown shortened season. The idea that Baylor would be good again post Rhule, after losing a large number of impact players to graduation and the NFL draft because they wore the same colors, ignored that those uniforms were now on different players. Consequently, with a new baseline of expectations set, no one had high expectations for Baylor in August of 2021. The Big 12 media collectively predicted them to finish 8th in a 10 team league. Was Aranda already on the hot seat? This preview's 2021 prediction that Aranda would fix the Bear defense and finish near the middle of the league with a 5-7 or 6-6 record seemed overly optimistic at the time!

Dave Aranda did more than just fix the defense in his second season. He also fired Larry Fedora and hired offensive coordinator Jeff Grimes from BYU to fix an awful Bear offense. Mission accomplished. The two coaches combined to realize, develop and nurture talent on the Baylor campus that no one knew was there. Like Matt Rhule before him, Aranda conjured a phoenix from the ashes and put six Bears into the NFL draft, the highest number of draft picks by any state of Texas program. The Bears improved their season win total by ten, going 12-2 and 7-2 in Big 12 play, won the Big 12 championship game starting their 2nd string quarterback, and handled a depleted Ole Miss easily in their bowl game. Aranda and his crew turned in the best coaching job in the nation. Aranda made some very poor initial hires, but his ability to immediately course correct on offense while simultaneously realizing the full vision of his defense in Year 2 was nothing less than masterful. The change in wins and season outcome tells the tale, but if you dig even deeper, Baylor transformed fundamentally to a shocking degree. An offense that averaged 4.4 yards per play in 2020 morphed to one that averaged 6.3 yards per play while returning only 4 offensive starters. The defense certainly also improved, rising from 61st to 9th nationally by advanced metrics, but without Jeff Grimes injecting enough offense, Baylor would not have achieved such a remarkable season. The proof? In 2020, Baylor was an atrocious 87th in the country on offense. In 2021, they finished a sneaky 10th in the nation by advanced metrics – Baylor played at a deliberative pace and did not create volume scoring and yards – on the strength of a running game that averaged 5.3 yards per carry and featured an opportunistic downfield passing game. That Grimes did it with Gerry Bohanon pulling the trigger for most of the year is even more remarkable.

Baylor's recent run also destroys the puzzlingly persistent sports notion that the world is immutable, teams never fall off or get better, or that nothing ever changes when you hire a new coach. These are the last five years of Baylor Bear football: 1-11, 7-6, 11-3, 2-7, 12-2. Horrendous, above average, great, horrendous, great. Starting with a nearly winless season under Matt Rhule, the Bears had a +6 win swing, a +4 win swing, a calamitous -9 win drop, and a +10 win swing in the span of four years. Waco emergency rooms were overwhelmed with whiplash victims every fall. It all adds up to a 33-29 five year record, an aggregate lie that suggests consistency and a middling program. Dave Aranda has built anything but a middling program in Waco, but there is another aggregate lie that prognosticators are using to forecast Baylor's 2022 fortunes: total returning starters. Baylor has the most of any team not named Kansas and, well, you know, that's Kansas. So given Baylor's 2021 title status, it stands to reason that they are the league's frontrunners, right? Pump the brakes on that. It's more complicated. Baylor is an ascendant program with very good coaching that may also be in need of a talent reload in some critical areas. How those two forces interplay will determine whether Baylor sees a whiplash decline to 7-5 or a retrenchment at the top at 10-2. A less than favorable road schedule may also pose a challenge. The Bears travel to BYU, Iowa State, Oklahoma, and Texas.

Strengths

6-7 310 pound Connor Galvin is probably the best offensive tackle in the Big 12. Deemed “too skinny” for Longhorn coaches coming out of high school, the 6-7, 260 pound Galvin shocked talent evaluators the world over by gaining size, weight, and strength by eating lots of food and lifting heavy weights while maturing from a boy to a man. Who knew that was possible? He is joined by fellow returning starter and former Buffalo transfer center Jacob Gall, who had the gall to transfer to Baylor and be much better than his MAC pedigree suggests. Beyond their MAC daddy center, big Khalil Keith has earned plenty of starts over his Bear career, but has yet to prove that he is a natural tackle. Mose Jeffery nabbed two starts last year but will need to prove he is up to snuff for an offensive line that did a tremendous job creating running lanes for Jeff Grimes' creative wide zone based rushing attack. Though Baylor has some good individual talents on the offensive line, their most impressive collective attribute is their cohesiveness and ability to cooperate seamlessly. A great example of how scheme can make players better.

The Baylor defensive front is stacked. Aranda's 4i based interior defensive front must thwart the opponent's running game for the rest of his machinations to work optimally and this unit projects to do just that. Perhaps even better than last year. Gabe Hall and TJ Franklin are big 295 pound interior defensive ends (Aranda likes to play them head up or inside the offensive tackle) who combined for 10 sacks last year while serving as rocks against the run. The biggest boulder inside is Siaki Ika. The 325 pounder is a load at nose tackle and he does a great job of freeing up Baylor's interior backers. Baylor also added an impact transfer in Tulsa's Jaxon Player. The squatty nose tackle can play with or alongside Ika and in relief of Franklin and Hall. Player totaled 31 tackles for loss and 8 sacks in four years at Tulsa and will have no problem integrating into the Bear rotation. That front is backed by the very physical Dillon Doyle at linebacker, who should contend for all-conference honors. The other linebackers are new faces, the most intriguing being perhaps LSU transfer Josh White.

It is odd to put a relatively unproven redshirt sophomore quarterback in the strength column but Blake Shapen is shapin' up to be a pretty promising player. Shapen beat out Gerry Bohanon this spring (Bohanon transferred to USF) after playing very promisingly for Baylor at the end of last season when Bohanon went down with an injury. The slightly built Shapen makes great decisions and Jeff Grimes loves his poise and ability to run the offense. Shapen carried the Bears to victory in the Big 12 title game, connecting on 23 of 28 throws for 180 yards and 3 touchdowns against a dangerous Oklahoma State offense, at one point hitting 17 completions in a row. He also threw for 254 yards and 2 touchdowns the week prior against Texas Tech. Shapen is clearly a passing game upgrade over Bohanon and if Baylor can add his accuracy to their creative play action offense, they will have the potential to make up for some significant skill talent losses at running back and wide receiver.

Weaknesses

Baylor's skill positions were gutted. Multipurpose runner Trestan Ebner finally exhausted his 17th year of eligibility (OK, perhaps an exaggeration) in Waco and was drafted by the Steelers. Abram

Smith came out of nowhere to have a dominant year, setting Baylor's single season rushing record with 1601 yards rushing at an impressive 6.2 yards per carry. Abram was an awesome fit for the Baylor running scheme and his no-nonsense style will be difficult to duplicate. Of course, given that Smith was a converted linebacker, perhaps Aranda can just produce record-breaking talent out of thin air on demand. They will have to do that at wide receiver, then. They lose #1 speedy wideout and 2nd round NFL draft pick Tyquan Thornton's 948 receiving yards and 10 touchdowns as well as #2 receiver RJ Sneed (46 catches, 573 yards) to a portal transfer to Colorado. #3 receiver Drew Estrada is also gone (30 catches). Sneed and Estrada are replaceable assets, but Thornton is not, and Baylor will miss their collective experience as much as their combined 138 catches. Returning from injury, Gavin Homes is the next most experienced receiver (he caught 33 balls underneath for a negligible yardage total back in 2020) and they will rely on unproven sophomores and freshmen to power their passing offense. One very big and bright spot returning is All-Big 12 TE Ben Sims, who grabbed six touchdowns last year on 31 balls. He may need to double that output for Baylor to have a solid passing game.

The sheer talent losses on the Baylor back end and at linebacker are severe. They lost four starters to the NFL draft. The idea that they will simply reload seems preposterous, but maybe Aranda's program is simply that good at development. Super safety Jalen Pitre went in the 2nd round of the draft after notching an incredible 18 tackles for loss and forcing five turnovers; big ranging safety JT Woods, who kept balls from going over the top of the Bear defense and nabbed 6 interceptions last year, went in the 3rd round; leading tackler and their most dynamic linebacker and blitzer (7.5 sacks) Terrel Bernard went in the 3rd to the Bills; finally, the Panthers took a flier on speed merchant cornerback Kalon Barnes late. Multiyear starter Raleigh Texada went undrafted. While big safety Christian Morgan and big cornerback Al Walcott will provide talent, stability and plenty of starting experience, the losses here cannot be discounted. Much of Baylor's elite play on defense was keyed by massive turnover generation and a back end that forced 27 takeaways via forced fumble and interception. Matching that statistic, no matter how much Aranda's clever schemes create those opportunities, seems improbable. Baylor's physical and well-drilled defense should be able to shut down opposing running games at will, but their matchups against higher end passing games could reveal some chinks in the armor.

In assessing schedule difficulty, when and where Texas plays their opponent matters. This is not a pure power ranking of each opponent on a neutral field played under perfect conditions in the middle of October. Alabama is the best opponent on the Longhorn schedule and the best team in the country. Kansas State, Oklahoma, Baylor and Oklahoma State represent the toughest conference matchups and the competition level takes a substantial step down after Kansas State.

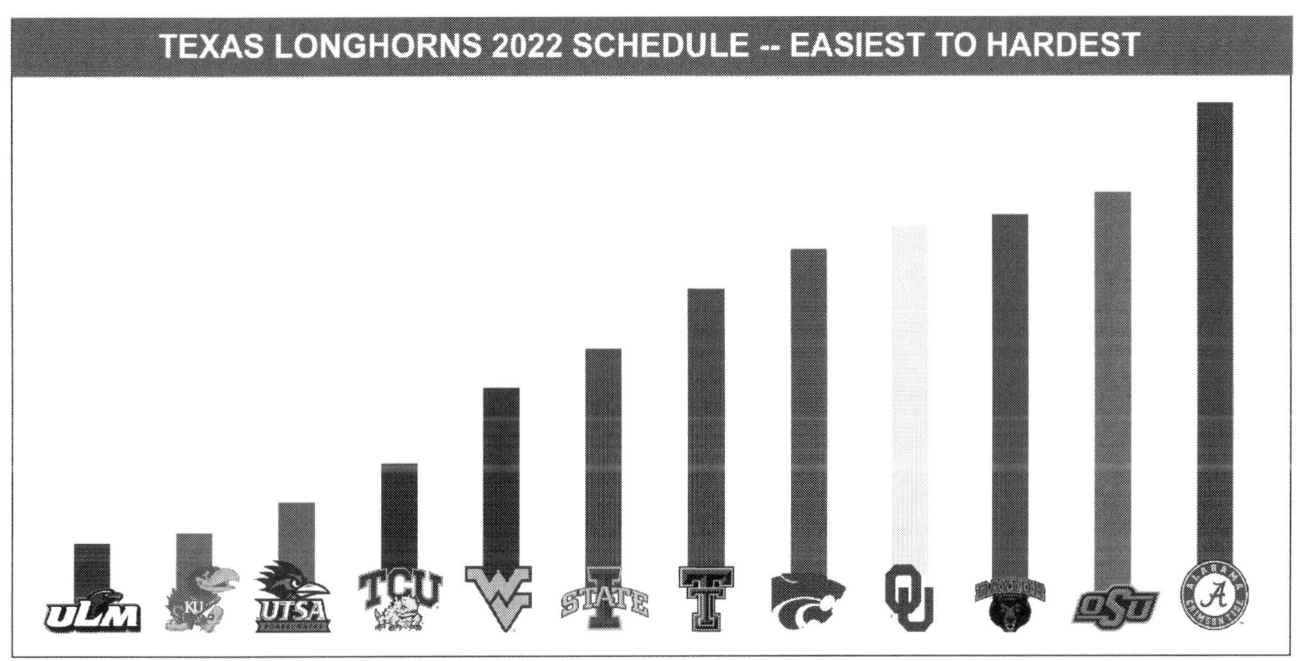

BIG XII CONFERENCE PREDICTIONS

Team	Wins	Losses
Oklahoma State	7	2
Texas	6	3
Baylor	6	3
Oklahoma	6	3
Kansas State	5	4
Iowa State	4	5
Texas Tech	4	5
West Virginia	3	6
TCU	3	6
Kansas	1	8

The Longhorns are fully capable of winning the Big 12. With more confidence in the offensive line and the defense, the preview would be very confident picking the Horns to boast the league's best record and potential double digit wins after the bowl season. Oklahoma is getting way too much carryover respect from national pundits predicting that they will win the league. In fact, 6-3 in league play may be too much respect. Oklahoma hired well, but Venables is stepping into a harder situation than most understand. Baylor and Oklahoma State deserve respect for their dominant defensive line play and outstanding coaching, but both have the potential to slip due to completely overhauling their linebacker and defensive back units. Baylor's offense also has some big question marks at the skill positions. Kansas State is an intriguing dark horse, but a lot of their tangible upside depends on their transfer quarterback from Nebraska. Iowa State, Texas Tech, TCU and West Virginia all have individually outstanding players and even high level individual units, but in totality, they have too many seeming headwinds. Kansas is a bad team, but Leipold is selecting the right types of competitors and fighters.

NFL DRAFT PICKS BY CONFERENCE

Conference	Draft Picks	Average/Team
SEC	65	4.64
Big Ten	48	3.43
Pac-12	25	2.08
Big XII	25	2.5
ACC	21	1.5
AAC	19	1.73
Mountain West	11	
MAC	6	
Conference USA	6	
Sun Belt	6	

The SEC continues to totally dominate the NFL talent share of college football. The Big 10 remains a firm #2 while the ACC's marked decline in NFL draft talent over the last couple of seasons is nothing less than shocking. The decline of Miami and Florida State, as well as a relatively poor season from Clemson, are primary contributors.

BIG XII CONFERENCE DRAFT PICKS	
Team	Picks
Oklahoma	7
Baylor	6
Iowa State	4
Oklahoma State	3
TCU	2
Texas Tech	2
Kansas State	2
Kansas	1
Texas	0
West Virginia	0

Texas was skunked in the 2022 NFL draft.

That's both an indicator of where the program has been, which Steve Sarkisian has little control over, but also a psychological obstacle to overcome when prospects and the fanbase take lagging indicators and project them forward. Sark and his staff are in the leading indicator business. That will come with success on the field in 2022, the ability to relate a vision of what can be, and having an affirmative culture of player development.

While some programs may get too much credit from the NFL, Texas seems to get very little of late. While understandable based on on-field results, a few individual Longhorn players undeservedly carried a larger program albatross that bore no relation to that individual's character or ability.

If Alabama players all have a halo, the Horns have had a hint of sulfur.

In fact, some of the better values found in the NFL draft have been Texas players that were undrafted free agents (Adrian Phillips, Poona Ford) or later round selections (DeShon Elliott, Charles Omenihu, Alex Okafor, Geoff Swaim).

Here are the raw numbers of the last decade of NFL Draft Selections at Texas:

Texas has averaged 2.5 NFL draft picks per year over the last decade, been skunked twice, and has had a high water mark of 5. Alabama had six first round draft picks last year alone. Texas has had two in the last decade (Vaccaro, Brown). The Cincinnati Bearcats just had nine players drafted. As many as the Horns over the last three years. Does recruiting matter? Indisputably. But development matters, too. In fact, through the proper lens, all aspects of the talent acquisition cycle are development. Recruiting is simply the first phase of the development process. The identification of raw material for the blueprint. The latter should drive the former, the process should be seamless, and not a distinct tasking. Far too often development is seen as a separate, disparate category. Recruiting is merely the antecedent of a bigger whole; the necessary start of the development process. Development doesn't begin when a player first steps on campus. It begins with the process of selection itself.

Where does Texas aspire? When Alabama played Georgia for the national title, there were 22 2022 NFL draftees playing. With several more prospects who will be featured prominently in the 2023 and 2024 NFL drafts. Since 2018, the On3 recruiting composite rankings rated Georgia and Alabama classes thusly:

2018: Georgia #1, Alabama #7

2019: Alabama #1, Georgia #2

2020: Georgia #1, Alabama #2

2021: Alabama #1, Georgia #3

Over the last four years, every year, either Georgia or Alabama finished #1 in recruiting. The two schools also finished #1 and #2 in aggregate recruiting over the last four years (Georgia is #1, Alabama a close #2), and the upperclassman core of Georgia's roster (the '18 and '19 classes) featured a total of fourteen 5 star recruits.

More importantly, both teams took that talent and developed it on and off of the field. Pure recruiting enthusiasts do not always like mention of the last part, eternally hoping that if their team has enough "talent" sitting around they will simply fall into a 13-1 season irrespective of program health, but the delta between recruiting rankings and on field performance *over large numbers* (i.e. not just one individual recruit) is more often explained by developmental failure than the evaluators getting it all wrong.Not all loaded teams will play for the national title, but the teams playing for the national title are always loaded with NFL draft talent.

2022 Recruiting Class

Special Guest Contributor Eric Nahlin

Despite a much slower summer of recruiting than expected followed by a disappointing 5-7 season, Steve Sarkisian and his staff were able to assemble a very strong top-5 recruiting class. The biggest factor was their patient, yet dogged approach. Patient meaning they didn't panic and reach for lesser prospects, while remaining dogged in their relationship building and self-confidence. It is true they had good fortune down the stretch with coaching changes, but that wouldn't have mattered if relationships didn't remain strong and they didn't retain vacancy in the class.

Despite team-wide failure in 2021, many of the coaches had excellent individual track records to sell, as well as playing time. Nowhere was that more evident than Kyle Flood and the offensive line class he signed. Sarkisian would go on to call it the best offensive line class ever signed, and offer it as exhibit A for why they chose not to add an offensive lineman through the portal.

At Inside Texas we don't just cover recruiting. We focus every bit as much on the team, and sometimes more depending on where we are in the calendar. Early returns are excellent on those linemen despite being on campus a short time. We've been told they believe they hit on each one relative to their individual expectations.

QB Maalik Murphy, Junipero Serra (Gardena, CA) – On3 Consensus: 91.30

Details: Every class has its share of boom or bust prospects and Murphy is probably No. 2 on that list behind Jaray Bledsoe. In no way is that a slight to Murphy, who by all accounts has terrific football character and character in general. He has the desire to be great and leadership intangibles. The other obvious positive trait going for him is arm talent, to mean both strength and also the ability to apply touch. Some guys who throw hard tend to always throw hard. While he arrives with a solid foundation he has to speed everything up about his delivery, from his feet to an arm action that is far too long. Can he move in the pocket, reset his feet, and get the throw off under duress? Another consideration perhaps working against him is timing of arrival at the program. This has affected so many quarterbacks both positively and negatively. Murphy finds himself sandwiched between Quinn Ewers and Arch Manning, two of the most highly rated quarterbacks of all time. Frequently kids make poor decisions and don't give themselves a chance to succeed — Murphy is the exact opposite. He's self-aware and works extremely hard. Despite the surrounding quarterback talent, he's going to give himself a chance, similar to fellow Steve Sarkisian quarterback Mac Jones at Alabama.

RB Jaydon Blue, Klein Cain (Houston, TX) – On3 C: 91.92

Details: Blue was one of the highest rated running backs in the country before he missed his senior year. Not playing, and the reasons for not playing, dropped him quite a bit in the rankings. However, the explosive ability, evidenced by 10.6 100 meter speed, has already shown up on campus. Though he missed his senior year, he was an early enrollee and participated in spring ball. He's more of a bounce and go runner than inside banger, but if the lane is there inside he has the quickness and speed to slash through. He also has terrific hands and can easily be motioned out to the slot. He'd be an interesting kick returner, maybe even ideal if he proves to be fearless.

OL Devon Campbell, Bowie (Arlington, TX) – On3 C: 98.08

Details: The five-star plays big and small at the same time. Small in the way he moves, big in the amount of space he takes up. Campbell's not the tallest but he's thick in his trunk and has decently long arms. The fact he could play defensive tackle in college, something his former high school coach mentioned about him, tells you how athletically gifted he is. He's also a pretty skilled basketball player and performed well in the throwing events in track and field. Despite not being an early enrollee, the staff is already encouraged by his ability. During his recruitment he said he wanted to try right tackle first and the staff has remained true to their word. Expect him to move inside, mainly because of one other freshman in particular. Regardless, this is a future pro and don't be surprised if he starts games this fall, though perhaps not immediately. That was our intel when he signed and it remains the case after a month of summer workouts.

OT Kelvin Banks, Summer Creek (Humble, TX) – On3 C: 97.22

Details: As much as I love Campbell, Banks was my personal No 1 player in the state for the class. He has come a long way since 9th grade which is evidence of his hard work to go along with his physical development. Texas has a huge question at left tackle that Banks is already working to answer. He is not only comfortable in pass protection, he run blocks with good leverage and intent. On top of everything, he's a high character kid — I lost count of how many of his coaches praised him at his All-America jersey ceremony. While attending that ceremony, Banks was committed to Oregon but the tea leaves were already blowing in UT's direction. Cristobal's departure opened the door for Texas to keep Banks home. Expect Banks to earn starts this season at left tackle and starting the opener isn't out of the question.

OT Cameron Williams, Duncanville (Duncanville, TX) – On3 C: 90.67

Details: Williams is a modern marvel who made a tremendous leap between his junior and senior year. At about 6-foot-5 and 370 pounds, you can't bull rush him or beat him inside. Surely he's not athletic enough against skilled outside pass-rushers, though? That's the craziest thing about him, he's probably better getting to his spot in pass protection than he is in the run game. One college coach intimately familiar with Williams and Banks thinks Williams has a higher upside. Early returns on him are strong and he's the most likely player of three options to become a right tackle in this class. The other two options being Campbell and Neto Umeozulu. He could conceivably unseat Christian Jones at some point this season.

OL Neto Umeozulu, Allen (Allen, TX) – On3 C: 94.42

Details: Assuming Williams becomes the right tackle of the future (2023 at the latest) that would put Umeozulu at guard which would be a great development as it's probably his best projection. Offensive line is about getting the five pieces in the right place and Umeozulu at guard would help do just that. Umeozulu has left tackle potential as a pass protector but he would be elite playing inside in that regard. His strength as a player, though, is winning position in the run game and keeping his feet moving. He has put on weight in the last six months and will likely play this season as a true freshman.

OL Malik Agbo, Todd Beamer (Federal Way, WA) – On3 C: 89.25

Details: I love that they were able to get Agbo in the class. I've seen lesser athletes play tackle in college and get drafted at guard. To be clear, he looks like a guard and will almost assuredly play there, but he plays with a surprising bounce for someone with his build. He hasn't played as much football as the other offensive lineman in the class, but he's not that far behind per sources.

IOL Cole Hutson, Frisco (Frisco, TX) – On3 C: 88.75

Details: Hutson was the only offensive line signee to enroll early and it definitely paid off for him as he received tons of reps and impressed during the spring. He's going to play this year, likely at guard, though he's also working at center this summer. He's a big guy who can move his feet and has the potential to become a very good interior player.

IOL Connor Robertson, Westlake (Austin, TX) – On3 C: 88.55

Details: Despite a lower rating, Robertson was one of Kyle Flood's first offers upon arriving in Austin. We know Flood likes his players big, and Robertson does have good size for center. To go along with size, he's a cerebral player which is a must for the position. He's the odds on favorite to be the starting center after Jake Majors.

WR Brenen Thompson, Spearman (Spearman, TX) – On3 C: 93.90

Details: Seldom do you see a 10.22 100 meter speedster also have a high floor but that's the case with Thompson. His play-speed was ridiculous in high school and was made even more comical by the competition he played. Though he missed most of his senior due to a foot injury, he returned healthy to the track and won state in the 100 meter with the time listed above and the 200 meter with a blistering 20.73. Texas will have its fastest group of receivers in a very long time, and Thompson is probably the fastest. He arrived under the assumption of being a slot, but he's showing generally good receiving skill this summer and may be more versatile than anticipated. He'll play as a freshman and will eventually get a chance to return punts and kicks.

WR Savion Red, Grand Prairie (Grand Prairie, TX) – On3 C: 83.65

Details: With Thompson in the slot you're hoping to go vertical with the passing game. When Savion Red is in the game, you're hoping to get him into a little bit of space and let his `running back' ability take over. He's not the athlete Jordan Whittington is, but the usage would be similar. Red moves well on the field but doesn't have great top-end speed. If he doesn't remain at receiver, he could play running back or even move to defense where safety or even linebacker could come into play. He is well known for being hyper-competitive whether under the lights or in the basketball gym.

EDGE Justice Finkley, Hewitt-Trussville (Hewitt, AL) – On3 C: 93.08

Details: With his powerful lower body and lower center of gravity he's going to force more than his share of pile-ups when the offense runs his way. He's both physically and mentally mature, but does have some length limitations. He is good off the ball and possesses good feet and balance, though he likely won't be a high sack player. As an early enrollee, expect Finkley to play this year given lack of depth at Edge. Texas is going to want to be bigger upfront this year, and Finkley, as the smallest guy on the D-line at times, would achieve that.

EDGE J'Mond Tapp, Ascension Catholic (Donaldsonville, LA) – On3 C: 92.90

Details: If you just look at where he's from and his rating you're probably wondering if you stumbled into an LSU season preview. But you're reading that right. Bo Davis still has the Midas touch and was able to land the very gifted Tapp. UT caught a bit of a break in that Tapp wanted to get some distance between himself and home in order to experience something different. Tapp is a sudden athlete with good feet. He plays with the type of balance you see in running backs. He seems an exceptional fit for Buck outside linebacker thanks to his ability to play forward and in reverse in coverage. He'll see the field this year, but how much remains to be seen.

EDGE Derrick Brown, Texas High (Texarkana, TX) – On3 C: 89.35

Details: Brown has the attributes to become a good pass rusher — he's good off the line and has good flexibility to get flat once the tackle is beaten. From the Edge, will he be able to box in the run? Probably, if given time. Ideally the staff is looking for a combination of Brown and Finkley.

EDGE Ethan Burke, Westlake (Austin, TX) – On3 C: 89.35

Details: Burke is a longer, leaner athlete with a sky-high ceiling. His lacrosse background is evident in the way he moves on the football field. Guys who are 6-foot-6 but move as well as Burke does omni-directionally are usually found on the basketball court. Burke could end up as the best pure pass rusher in the class, but he'll need a year to develop. He was set to sign with Michigan until Texas wisely swooped in and flipped him.

LB Trevell Johnson, Martin (Arlington, TX) – On3 C: 88.50

Details: Johnson missed his senior year due to a hip injury. Similar to his former Martin teammate, Morice Blackwell, Johnson may get a look at safety despite being considered a linebacker. He is on a longer developmental curve. He knows the game, but will require physical development.

DL Jaray Bledsoe, Marlin (Marlin, TX) – On3 C: 92.90

Details: Never mind the rating, it's merely an average of his boom or bust potential. He's perhaps the most talented prospect in the class. After being forced to sit out his senior year due to a UIL transfer ruling, he enrolled early at Texas where his physical ability was obvious from the word go. Unfortunately, his spring was derailed after only a handful of practices when he needed to have his appendix removed. Though he profiles to the interior long term, his length and raw athleticism will have the coaches trying him at defensive end as a freshman to address an obvious roster need. Because of his athleticism, he could probably play long- term, but that wouldn't be his best fit. He's similar to Alfred Collins in that regard.

DL Kristopher Ross, North Shore (Houston, TX) – On3 C: 92.03

Details: North Shore has produced some knuckleheads, but that's not the personification of program culture on the east side. Guys like Kristopher Ross are. His motor runs hot with many tackles being made very far from his alignment. He's going to buy-in and work. He's a little undersized to the point I wonder if he'll play defensive end, but what weight he adds will be functional. We know that because what weight he has now is highly functional. He threw the shot put over 60 feet as a junior. He was the Houston Touchdown Club's defensive player of the year after living in the back field all season.

DL Aaron Bryant, Southaven (Southaven, MS) – On3 C: 90.00

Details: Bryant is going to become a quality role player at a minimum, but he'll need time for the depth chart to thin in front of him. The early enrollee was known to be a hard worker before arriving in Austin and that has held true. He doesn't have a prototypical build, looks more like a high-end guard, but he's strong and can move his feet. Maybe not a special player, but he has the potential to be a good one.

DL Zac Swanson, Brophy College Preparatory (Phoenix, AZ) – On3 C: 88.03

Details: Swanson's father was a quality offensive lineman at Stanford. He's a good student, but not Stanford good which opened the door for Texas and Oregon. He played the edge in high school but will likely spin down to 3-tech in college. He lacks ideal length, but does have strong hands and a great first step. If you're going to overcome length concerns, that's how you do it, along with moving inside to face guards rather than tackles.

S B.J. Allen Jr., Aledo (Aledo, TX) – On3 C: 93.13

Details: When Tom Herman arrived at Texas he soon flipped Caden Sterns from LSU. A sign Herman's tenure wasn't going great was when Allen Jr., who was primed for Texas, chose LSU. History repeated itself when Steve Sarkisian was able to get a commitment from Allen Jr not long after he decommitted from LSU. A certain former TCU head coach is said to be very high on Allen, who started to come on later in spring ball. He's a versatile defender but his thicker build will land him at boundary safety, where he'll get to support the run and freelance some. Opposing coaches who won State raved about Allen Jr after playing Aledo. Don't expect him to start this year, but the following year boundary safety will be his position to lose.

S Larry Turner-Gooden, Bishop Alemany (Playa Del Rey, CA) – On3 C: 89.42

Details: Turner-Gooden burst on the scene as a sophomore but then was limited as a junior and senior due to Covid policies and injuries. He may have lost some athleticism in the process but he gave himself a chance by enrolling early and going through spring ball. He's a bigger body and instinctive, which means boundary safety could be a fit if he's athletic enough. If not, a move to linebacker could be his best bet to make an impact. Of course a move like that brings with it a number of questions, with the most important being, does he have the mentality for it?

CB Terrance Brooks, Little Elm (Little Elm, TX) – On3 C: 95.53

Details: Flipping the early enrollee from Ohio State at the 11th hour was a coup for corners coach Terry Joseph. On3 had Brooks rated a five-star in large part to his very high floor. If cornerback doesn't work out, then he could become an exceptional Star or safety. His father, Chet, had an NFL All-Pro season as a San Francisco 49er. Brooks has already added a lot of weight since arriving in college. He's almost unrecognizable from the time his recruitment started. That means a move to safety might be inevitable, but that could be a good thing. Improved talent at safety is a roster need.

CB Jaylon Guilbeau, Memorial (Port Arthur, TX) – On3 C: 92.55

Details: As an early enrollee, Guilbeau had an interesting spring. The hard work and football acumen he was known for received frequent praise, while the poor decision-making away from the field he wasn't known for reared its head twice. Neither infraction was terrible on its own, but when occurring within weeks of each other it is cause for mild concern. Guilbeau is physical, smart, and generally possesses corner traits. Long-speed has been the question but as of this writing there are no plans to move him to Star or safety. He probably projects to Star best, but you're a corner until you aren't.

CB Austin Jordan, Ryan (Denton, TX) – On3 C: 91.10

Details: You want prospects who play their best football as seniors. You'd think that's always the case, but it's not. Jordan, however, had by far his most impressive campaign from an evaluation standpoint. He's given himself a better chance to remain at cornerback. His physicality was always apparent, but was he athletic enough? Tape of him moonlighting at wide receiver was encouraging. A move is probably still the most likely outcome, but he could emerge as one of the steals of the class. Ryan coaches rave about his football character.

CB Xavion Brice, Seguin (Arlington, TX) – On3 C: 88.38

Details: It's always a good sign when the more lower rated recruits in a class earned their offer after attending camp. That's exactly what happened with Brice, not only at Texas, but also Oklahoma where he originally committed. Texas was able to flip him after Lincoln Riley departed for Southern Cal. As a player, Brice is viewed as a potential corner, but likely field safety. He possesses good fluidity and ball skills but not the long speed for cornerback. Star is a possibility as well. If you're noticing a trend of potential corners, but probable safeties or nickels, that's by design. The coaches are selecting for coverage ability first and foremost.

K Will Stone, Regents School (Austin, TX) – On3 C: 80.88

Details: He's similar to recent Austin kicking product Cameron Dicker who just finished his career at Texas. The big difference, Stone is left footed. Stone may have a stronger leg with the ability to kick a 54 yarder in high school and send his kicks well out of the back of the end zone. Like Dicker, he's also a good punter. Kicking duties are up for grabs but it's such a mental position it's impossible to know how soon Stone will be ready to perform in front of 100,000 people.

LS Lance St. Louis, Williams Field (Gilbert, AZ) – On3 C: 78.12

Details: His father Brad St. Louis was drafted by the Cincinnati Bengals in the seventh round of the 2000 NFL draft.

Arch Madness: The Perfect Storm of Recruitment

Contributor: Eric Nahlin

A team that goes 5-7 has no business landing the nation`s No 1 prospect, let alone the latest model from the Manning family quarterback assembly line, right? I forgive anyone who thought Inside Texas was off its rocker for covering this recruitment so earnestly, but anyone who read this site understood this development was possible for myriad, complementary reasons.

It starts with the Mannings and their general fondness for the school. We knew Cooper Manning almost went to UT, and then more famously Eli Manning nearly did as well. But what really caught our attention was when we learned how close Cooper and Ellen Manning were to sending their daughter May to UT. Okay, so now we know the family's fondness extended into the younger generation. Interesting. I would go on to find out how well Cooper fit in with a subset of Texas-ex businessmen, mostly living in Dallas. I knew he had friends all over — and would later learn that extended to Georgia alums — but these were relationships that went well beyond business.

That's all fine and well, but Cooper went to Ole Miss like his father and brother and surely his son will do the same. That's not what the early information led us to believe. Early on it wasn't so cut and dried Ole Miss wouldn't be a factor, but it was clear long before Arch would pick his school. So maybe there's a chance, but the Mannings aren't going to let Tom Herman turn Arch into a Zamboni like they did Sam Ehlinger, so the story was on hold. When Steve Sarkisian replaced Tom Herman, the story came out of the deep freeze to thaw. Almost immediately after Sark was hired I had people calling me to say how big this could be for Arch. Arch? At the time I was focused on Quinn Ewers but the details *were* interesting. IT learned the Mannings viewed Sark as a top-five offensive mind in college football and it was pretty clear Arch wouldn't be playing for any of the other four.

We put that story on the small burner to simmer until Quinn Ewers picked Ohio State when we turned up the heat. Arch visited Texas in the summer of 2021. He was off a recent Clemson visit that produced a ton of buzz, but the end result was they really liked Dabo Swinney and the school setting, but the offense made it a no-go. Meanwhile the Texas visit went very well and Sarkisian was already pulling consensus building levers between Arch and a handful of top prospects.

As summer ended Clemson was mostly out, if not entirely. Ole Miss was already out. LSU was a non-factor. As Arch began his junior year, this race narrowed down to Texas, Georgia, and Alabama, even if many didn't realize it.

That brings us to that 5-7 record. No matter how much the Mannings liked Sark, relationships wouldn't be enough to seal it, right? No, that wasn't enough, but Texas had so many other factors going for it. Here are just a few:

The staff Sark assembled was very well suited to work as a team and win this recruitment. Along with Sark's reputation for offense and quarterback development, AJ Milwee's demeanor and personality was seen as a perfect fit for Arch (and the coaches at Isidore Newman, who he struck deep bonds with).

Said one source of Milwee, "Because I want to make sure he gets his laurels, the relationship between Arch and AJ Milwee is the strongest of any head coach, coordinator or QB coach at any school that recruited Arch, including Sark (who clearly did a phenomenal job). I know you probably know this but I'm not sure this happens without Milwee."

The source continued, "Absolutely phenomenal relationship builder. Got very close with Arch and Cooper. Incredibly consistent communicator and extremely authentic. Does a great job of making QB recruits feel like they are already being coached by him in recruiting meetings and is a very good teacher. Has enough wisdom to be respectable but comes off as young enough to relate to guys. He's reserved but very likable in a 1 on 1 setting. Makes it clear he will coach his guys hard. I'd like to play in his room."

On top of that, cornerbacks coach Terry Joseph played a key introductory role and always had his ear to the street. The same source on Joseph, "Terry Joseph played a big part as well. Very connected to NOLA as everyone knows, very well respected in that area. He was one of the primary communicators with Cooper, very consistent on that front and did a good job of staying plugged in throughout. Less important with Arch, more so with family/coaches."

You have to approach recruitments in a way that is custom fit to the recruit's personality and Texas, with the help of Joseph, did just that.

Also assisting was Kyle Flood. He took a more prominent role in the recruitment after his fantastic offensive line haul, which itself was a key factor.

Texas had campus life in its favor. Arch doesn't want the attention that comes with playing the quarterback position at a major school. Factor in his last name and it's even more difficult to blend in. The bigger environment of Austin, which reminded him of New Orleans, benefitted the school.

To say nothing negative of Georgia, academics benefitted the school as well. It was refreshing to hear how much education mattered. They were taking nothing for granted with Arch and the NFL. Perhaps Cooper's own injury history and success in the real world gave him such a good perspective.

While Cooper had so many good relationships with Texas-exes, Arch has a number of strong relationships with current Texas students. Every time he visited we heard how comfortable he was on campus — and also how normal he was.

Quinn Ewers' reclassification was big. It's freaking unreal Texas will have both on the roster. That would not have happened without Ewers reclassifying. Sark played that well, by the way. He was honest and upfront with the Mannings about the pursuit of Ewers, but made it clear Quinn wasn't going to be on campus all that long.

If you felt Occam's razor was `Georgia good, Texas bad' you were going to be wrong from the start. It could have just as easily been comparing Kirby Smart's quarterback track record to Steve Sarkisian's.

In the end the Mannings made a holistic decision, and the school was set up well to win because of a perfect storm of factors.

About the Authors/Creators

Paul Wadlington is a Texas graduate, Amazon best selling author, podcaster, partner in a financial business, commercial real estate investor and inveterate entrepreneur currently living in Colorado Springs, Colorado. Paul is a contributor at Inside Texas and the co-founder of Barking Carnival and the FanTake network. Make sure to listen to the Everyone Gets A Trophy podcast wherever you listen to your podcasts. Feel free to reach out to Paul at trophymailbag@gmail.com

Will Gallagher is a talented professional photographer, Austin native and Texas graduate whose work can be found at http://gallagherstudios.com. Will provided the incredible photos that enrich this preview.

Eric Nahlin is a recruiting industry expert, Longhorn insider, and the managing partner at Inside Texas. He lives in Houston. Use Promo Code TTFIT22 for 50% off of Inside Texas for one year. That's $50 for a year of the best Longhorn and football content in the universe.

**

If you enjoyed the read, please let others know and rate and review wherever you bought it. Your support is vital in allowing us to create a great product. Thanks for Thinking Texas Football with us and please support our sponsors.

The Gabe Winslow Mortgage Team
832-557-1095
www.mortgagesbygabe.com
Remember, promo code: THINKING TEXAS. Hook 'em.

Made in the USA
Columbia, SC
08 February 2023